Only on the Bus

School Bus Tales and Folklore

By

Jason R. Dunkelberger

Acknowledgements

Heartfelt thanks to my beloved wife, Lisa, and my loving children, Isabel, Emily, Conner, and Olivia. A special thanks to Lisa, Aisha, and Misty.

Dedication

This book is dedicated to James Pinder, a kind and considerate bus driver, who genuinely cared for his children and everyone he worked with, providing student transportation.

Disclaimer

This is a work of fiction. Names, characters, businesses, places, events, and incidents are either the products of the author's imagination or used in a fictitious manner. Any resemblance to actual persons, living or dead, or actual events is purely coincidental.

Preface

Providing a better understanding of how student transportation runs behind the scenes was a difficult task without including an array of short stories and hilarious experiences. For years, the idea of writing a book to better describe the bus driving profession seemed daunting, yet the pages multiplied as the hilarious stories kept coming back into my mind. Our school buses are a mode of transportation the entire community depends on, with bus drivers, we unquestionably trust to transport our most precious gifts from God. Although the characters in this book are fictitious, the stories have been derived from real-world experiences and incidents that have occurred over my years of education. Writing from multiple views of different aspects of student transportation can be enjoyable. Explaining how parents, students, teachers, bus drivers and administrators interact can be both comical and tragic. There is indeed a bright side and a dark side of student transportation. Giving my heart and soul to show others how absolutely amazing our school bus drivers can be is my pleasure and my intent.

Introduction

Have you ever wondered what goes on inside those big, yellow school buses every morning? As the sun rises each day, there are a group of individuals who grab a cup of coffee, put a smile on their face, and are the very first people from a school district to greet your children. Student transportation is a rewarding profession where an array of individuals come to work twice a day to drive students to and from school. They are parents, grandparents, retired, and veterans. They love kids. Serve as teachers, coaches, mentors, and confidants to the youth of today. With technology and social media clogging up natural experiences and good parenting with inappropriate content and profane ideology, children struggle to define good morals, values, and discipline in their daily routines.

Bus drivers are the very first and last members of a school district to see and speak to student bus riders. They start with a smile, hold our children accountable for doing what is right even when nobody's looking, and watch over their students' safety and well-being like guardian angels.

Our student transportation professionals are advocates for emotional support, social understanding, and physical protection. They stand up to inappropriate behavior and harassment. They teach empathy and kindness. Most importantly, they love and care for your children.

Take a moment and share a few days on the school bus. Learn through the eyes of our bus drivers how our children act, react, and develop on the school bus, similar to the classroom.

Table of Contents

Chapter 1
Morning Route

Opening the door at the crack of dawn, I smile as I watch a bright pink jacket come aboard my school bus with rosy cheeks and a glimmering smile.

Cynthia is a kindergartner I pick up from an apartment complex just south of town. Cynthia is one of four children in the Rosales family. She is a quiet child who sings songs and views going to school each day as an adventure.

"Good morning, Cynthia!" I exclaim.

"Morning Mr. Russell!" she mumbles as she hops into her booster seat in the second row. Her older sister heads to the back of the school bus, holding a thermal cup of coffee and looking at her phone. She doesn't say a word, as I have learned, she is definitely not a morning person.

Starting out, I pick up children from the Lake Andrews apartment complex south of town and wind my way around the county. I pick up elementary children until I reach capacity, then head to the two elementary schools to drop off my first load of children.

Johnny Williams and Chris Douglas hop aboard my bus on my second stop each morning. Both students are carrying their backpacks and joking back and forth about playing video games together the night before. Johnny is a fifth grader, tall, skinny, and short brown hair. Johnny lives on a small ranch, and his father works in the oil fields.

Even though his father is out of town, Johnny is a good young man, and he answers to his mother without question.

He has two older brothers in high school. They are disciplined as well. I pick them up later on my secondary route.

On my next stop, Adam Adkins lives in a small house with his mother. Adam's father died of cancer a few years ago, and his mother seems to work all the time. Adam has excellent manners like Johnny and is always pleasant. Adam seems to look up to Johnny and his older brothers. Adam is a bit introverted, but he opens up when he is around his friend, Johnny.

It did take a while, after his father passed, to get Adam to talk again. Both boys are great on the bus and seldom cause any drama. I enjoy watching their friendship develop and their consistent comradery.

As we pass under the old oak trees stretching across the road, we turn down Locust Street to pick up three children.

Anna, Julia, and Adam Rodgers live in a small blue house near Big Creek. They are all cute as a button and are originally from outside of Nashville, Tennessee.

Their mother moved into our district in the middle of the school year, escaping from an extremely, abusive relationship. Ms. Rodgers receives financial support from the State of Texas and her children remain under the protection of Child Protective Services.

Ms. Rodgers struggles with severe physical and mental abuse she received from her ex-husband. Her ex-husband was finally incarcerated in Tennessee after years of domestic violence. Ms. Rodgers is extremely protective of her children and is always mindful of their health and welfare.

Anna is her fifth grader, skinny, long, braided, brown hair, and seems to serve as the protector of the group. Anna is quick to correct her siblings and guide them to and from school each day.

Julia is the second grader, short, blond hair, and quiet as a mouse. She seems afraid to talk to anyone other than her mother and her older sister. It took a long while to get her to even respond to my morning greeting.

Adam is a kindergarten student, stocky, young man with dark, brown hair. Adam doesn't seem to have a care in the world and often struggles with staying in his seat. He is always silly and quite mischievous.

As for Ms. Rodgers, she is a short, skinny woman who is always wearing a ball cap and a sun dress. Her clothes are frayed, outdated, and sometimes soiled. She smiles, a cigarette in one hand and a steaming cup of morning sunshine in the other.

I must say Ms. Rodgers seems a bit stressed. She has a raspy voice and is always talking about keeping her "babies" safe. She has several scars on her arms and a large scar across her left cheek.

As I push my parking brake in, I can only imagine how much she must have endured in her previous relationship.

Driving across a small bridge, we approach a beautiful white ranch house, set in the middle of a rolling pasture. A herd of black Angus watches our school bus drive by like an attentive audience in a theater as we pull up to a black steel gate at the end of a driveway.

A new, white, dually pickup truck is idling by the entrance as two children hop out of the back door and grab their belongings. A man wearing a cowboy hat, seated in the driver's seat, waves as I close the bus doors and start towards our next stop.

I honk my horn, wave, and proceed.

A few miles later, we begin a series of stops in a small subdivision. The children quickly load as I drive from stop to stop. Most kids move quickly to their seats to see their friends once again or get back on their cell phones to continue their game.

Almost 60 elementary children are loaded onto my school bus every morning, an average for my primary route.

Mornings are often quiet and our school bus is usually full of students on their cell phones and other electronic devices to pass time.

Those who aren't on their cell phones are chatting among themselves. Some children are sound asleep.

Victor is out cold after only a few minutes in his seat.

The boy can sleep through a tornado!

He is in second grade and a chubby little fellow. Victor is always sneaking snacks out of his backpack on his way to his seat. No matter how many times I ask him to put it away, the boy keeps eating.

Periodically, I remind students to sit down or stay in their assigned seats to keep everyone safe. Sometimes, I feel like I am talking to myself; however, they do have the best chance of surviving an accident if they are seated forward. At least, that is what they tell me!

However, trying to stop kids from eating on the school bus is nearly impossible. Every evening, there is a collection of candy wrappers, pencils, and lunch boxes when I sweep out my school bus. If I don't, I know "Ricky the Raccoon" will be on my bus in the morning!

Ricky is an exceptionally chubby raccoon for a reason!

Some folks assume we can see every child in our big rearview mirrors. Let me tell ya, our seats are so tall, you could pretty much do anything you want back there, and we would have no idea!

It's our camera surveillance that captures most of the horseplay and rule violations.

When I am driving, I can't see most of the children unless they are hanging in the aisle or not sitting down. When I have to give the kids constant reminders, it makes the ride unpleasant. But, better safe than sorry!

We arrive at our first campus, and I see Mr. Stanley, the Assistant Principal of Manor Elementary School in his Sunday's best. He is a tall man, medium build, with a beard and short brown hair. He is wearing a sports jacket and a collared shirt.

Mr. Stanley has been in education for fifteen years and keeps the campus running smoothly for over 450 elementary students. Mr. Stanley is married and has four children of his own. His wife is the campus librarian at the middle school.

Over half of my riders get off at Manor Elementary School. After dropping children at each elementary campus, a sense of accomplishment fills my heart! I enjoy serving our district and taking so many children to school each day.

I love my job, and I enjoy being the very first person each child sees on their way to school every day!

"Why do I get up so early each day, you ask?"

"For the kids!" should be the only answer we give as bus drivers; because, anything else is a lie!

Chapter 2
Inappropriate Language

After dropping my elementary children off at the first elementary school, I drive three miles to Alexander Elementary School and drop the remainder of my kids off. Usually, Ms. Tate is standing on the curb waiting for us to arrive.

She is a kind, older lady who often wears vibrant outfits for the kids. She always seems happy and tries to greet every child as they each step onto the curb by their name. She has over 400 children, and she knows them all.

Leaving Alexander Elementary, I begin the second portion of my morning route, picking up my secondary students. Some drivers haul only primary students, while others haul only secondary. I have a mirrored route, and essentially, I pick up the young children and later their big brothers and sisters.

When the school district decided to split our routes into elementary and secondary groups, our Director was excited because he believed the complaints would subside and he could finally enjoy a little peace and quiet.

Mr. Danforth wouldn't have to explain why a parent's elementary-aged child was using profanity at the dinner table and asking about adult topics.

It didn't take long for the district leadership to recognize the need to separate primary and secondary on our school buses.

The previous school year, Mr. Danforth received countless complaints from parents claiming their young children were learning profane language and racial slurs on the school bus. Parents were pushing to make a change.

As you can imagine, most parents were horrified when their child dropped a colorful expletive after refusing to eat their vegetables.

Although we sit at home and forget what words roll out of our mouths around our own children, bus drivers really do try to make an honest attempt to foster a clean, safe learning environment on their school buses.

Some would say we actually protect childhood innocence by fostering a wholesome, age-appropriate environment for our children. After all, we are truly trusted officials in our community to do what is best for kids.

As bus drivers, we try to advocate for our children and are extremely protective of their innocence. With middle school and high school students on our school buses, it can be a challenge to stop the profane language and the inappropriate topics kids choose to discuss from entering young, innocent elementary ears.

We may try to correct them, call their parents, and even turn in discipline reports to try to change the older kids' behavior; but stopping it sometimes seems impossible without beating them or using shock collars. Apparently, those methods are frowned upon.

Holding children accountable involves parental support, strong assistant principals taking care of student discipline, and bus drivers staying consistent with the enforcement of the rules on their school bus.

"My parents don't care that I cuss!" a female high school student arrogantly responded. "They cuss, too!"

Explaining the use of profanity as a replacement for a lack of vocabulary goes in one ear and out the other to the typical child.

Don't even try telling middle and high school children they are not adults; therefore, they should not use profanity. You're asking for a barrage of derogatory comments that lead to nowhere fast!

Threatening kids with disciplinary action will only work if you actually do it.

Then again, if you make threats too much, you may fall on deaf ears similar to the boy who cried wolf.

Ignoring profanity doesn't solve the problem either and can be problematic when a second grader attempts to use the same colorful language at home, and then Dad calls to ask you why his second grader is using profanity he learned on the school bus.

It's funny; the Dad will cuss like a sailor the entire phone call during his complaint at whoever answers, but never acknowledges the profanity may be originating from his colorful vocabulary.

Rest assured, Dad will demand immediate response to this travesty and the man may never realize he may be the source of the profane language himself.

As I get older, I find profanity is more and more evident in television shows and blockbuster movies. My skin crawls when a movie script requires a young child to use profanity.

It just doesn't seem right to me. Together, we all need to keep our children appropriate and respectful.

A coach once mentioned, "We need to allow our children to learn life's lessons with consequences!"

"Teaching right from wrong has to be memorable; otherwise, they never truly learn the lesson."

Well said, Coach.

Please make sure you don't cuss on the football field, either! All credibility is lost with a double standard.

Sometimes, our children are our best representation of what is right and just.

Julio Ramos, a tall, distinguished young man, lives at the end of a gravel road. His family owns a ranch and raises cattle. One day, Julio's parents offered their enormous driveway to turn my school bus around earlier in the school year. It is so much easier than driving down another three miles to turn around the bus.

They are a great family, and I look forward to seeing them every morning. I always make sure to smile and wave when they are standing outside with their kids, drinking their morning coffee.

Now, Julio will quickly correct any student on the school bus who uses profanity or threatens a younger child. He is well-spoken, respectful, and pleasant to have on my school bus. His ability to influence the kids in a positive way is encouraging to see.

After leaving the Ramos Ranch, Penelope and Piper Chamberlin are my next stop. They are twin girls in high school who constantly bicker on a daily basis.

If it isn't about makeup or the latest fashion, they are on their phones, finding things to show each other and giggling. It's funny how our children have lost the art of verbal communication but easily share in socializing over social media and text.

Yesterday, I asked a student to sit down and the student ignored my instructions!

"Are you sure they heard you?" I thought to myself.

"No, they had those white earphones in their ears and gave me a dirty look!" I said to myself.

You know, people pay good money to sit in a restaurant and enjoy each other's company. Have you noticed everyone's on their cell phones before, sometimes during, and even after their meal?" Technology can be consuming.

Years ago, kids would talk and laugh and giggle the entire ride to school. Some children would misbehave, but most students would enjoy the ride to school.

Now, children have difficulty communicating with each other and become dependent on their electronic devices and social media.

Some have actually been recommended to attend counseling sessions to learn how to interact with others because they are so engrained in their electronics and never took the time to communicate.

Complaining about electronic devices may confirm how old a bus driver may be; however, some children are also not fortunate enough to have one, especially elementary children. They seem to have the most fun on the school bus.

Jimmy Jones doesn't have a cell phone. His family lives in a run-down mobile home on the edge of town. Although he does not have a phone himself, Jimmy is constantly trying to look over the seats of other kids on their phones.

I do catch Jimmy trying to take other children's cell phones for a few minutes to play a game or surf the internet. The little guy always struggles to give it back. I often have to tell him to return the phone to the child it belonged to before they get upset.

He eventually returns the item, but you can tell he is disappointed.

Although Jimmy really loves electronics, he is a friendly young man. His parents struggle financially to keep food on the table, and Jimmy's father is extremely skeptical of the internet. A conspiracy theorist of sorts.

Make no mistake, Jimmy's mother works tirelessly raising five children and does a great job taking care of them all. Jimmy is a brilliant boy and will talk your ear off if you give him an opportunity.

He sits on the passenger side front seat willingly and will talk the entire way to school if you let him. Sometimes, I wish I could give him my phone to catch a break in the conversation.

Most children dread sitting up front, but Jimmy loves to look out of the front window and chat with anyone who will listen.

He can tell you every stop if you are a substitute driver, and he knows every child on the school bus by name. I believe someday, Jimmy will be a very successful man.

Driving into the valley, Bella Christiansen's stop is next. Bella is a band child and often struggles to hold her backpack, clarinet, lunch box and whatever else she decides to bring to school as she walks onto the school bus and back to her seat.

Bella is a quiet 10th grader who rarely makes a peep. She often looks out of the window and may catch a nap in the mornings before school. I believe Bella has quite a bit of pressure on her by her parents. She always looks so exhausted.

Bella lives in a middle-class subdivision, and she waits for the school bus in front of their beautiful home.

I have never seen her parents and there are seldom vehicles in her driveway. I would suspect she is a latchkey child since both parents work extended hours. Dual-employment families are common in this neighborhood.

We continue to drive through the Crystal Falls subdivision, picking up numerous children. A high school student named Timothy Owens seems to turn up the volume on the entire school bus when he gets on the bus.

Timothy can be loud and obnoxious. He will speak to the children on the bus as a group, make statements for all the children to hear, and drop more profane language than a sailor at sea.

Timothy is an athlete and sits in the back of the school bus with two other boys. He wears designer clothes, a concerning amount of bad cologne, and a ball cap backwards on his head.

Michael Kuhns and Eddie Perez sit across from Timothy. All three boys live in Crystal Falls, and their parents have large homes. After the three boys join forces, nobody on the school bus is safe from their ridicule and eminent, profane comedy show.

In the short period of time before drop off at school, the boys begin their daily routine of talking loudly, harassing nearby students, and chomping on their bubble gum.

Sometimes, I can't wait to get to the high school.

Chapter 3
Trusted Influence

After assuming this new route earlier this year, it is easy to see that the last bus driver let the children go and never truly established any rules or norms.

The elementary children are a blessing. The secondary students who lack respect and discipline turn my school bus into a rolling circus.

As a school bus driver, we are taught that we are an extension of a typical classroom. Meaning we must maintain a safe learning environment for every child just like the school campuses.

I truly believe this is a great analogy because our children are like little sponges. Especially our young riders, who listen and are more attentive than you can imagine.

Even though students try to avoid turmoil on the school bus, bullies still extend their ridicule onto the school bus. I am thankful we have the administrative support to submit discipline reports that result in real disciplinary consequences for children who are being mean to the other children on the school bus.

If you don't have administrative support, you will quickly find yourself feeling alone, and that's not good for anyone, especially the children riding on your school bus.

Our children need protection from the vicious harassment and intolerable treatment some children can unload on them.

Before cameras, telling the bus driver or your teacher was the way kids reported wrongdoing. Now, the cameras catch the students' actions, and every seat is thankfully protected by video surveillance.

The best part is knowing the kids are not going to get blamed for "snitching" on someone. The video surveillance can always be the scapegoat for reporting bad behavior.

Different school districts handle discipline on school buses in different ways. As a bus driver, you are often driving on busy roads and clearly have the safety of everyone onboard in your hands.

We have to focus on the road, accommodate the countless drivers speeding past our school bus, and keep everyone safe when things don't go our way. It is simple, right?

"That is Bus Driver 101. Your first lesson learned.

Sounds easy, right?

Now, as a new driver, consider two children fighting in the back of your bus. Perhaps a child is screaming bloody murder right behind you. Pulling up to a bus stop, a parent comes to your door and provides a profane description of how you should be a better driver or arrive earlier.

"How does a normal human being handle these challenges, you say?"

A bus driver may ask themselves, "Why is he so mean?" as he yells at them at the crack of dawn.

Go back in the house or take your kids to school yourself might be a thought.

But what bus drivers are really hoping a parent will say is simple.

"Thank you!"

Bus drivers are trusted representatives of the school district, professionals who have the ability to report abuse and neglect, and surprisingly, most are even parents with children and grandchildren of their own.

We should remember that they have a great deal of influence over our children, and they do their best to take care of them.

Not every day is miserable on a school bus. Actually, we enjoy most days driving kids back and forth to school!

Every morning, I pick up Hector and his sister Helen after we leave the subdivision. Hector is a stocky young man with wavy black hair, and Helen is a chubby girl with pink glasses. Both children walk across their front yard while the family dogs bark at the school bus.

Hector stops to let his sister board the school bus first and follows her to their seats. "Good Morning, Mr. Russell!" Hector says as he smiles and pats me on the shoulder.

"Good morning, Hector!"

"Good Morning, Ms. Helen!"

Helen quietly goes to her seat. She is a bit introverted.

When both children are seated, we pull off.

We drive along the county road and look to see a few buzzards eating a deer carcass. As the school bus gets closer, the buzzards fly up onto a tree limb and keep watch over their morning meal.

The leaves on the oak trees are turning a beautiful maroon and rust color, signifying fall is here! The sunrise is breathtaking in the Texas sky.

Approaching a country railroad crossing, the lights begin to flash, and I bring the school bus to a stop. A freight train passes by, and the children in the back begin counting the rail cars.

Two children mention the graffiti on the railcars and talk about what they would draw if given the opportunity.

The black and white crossing rail raises as the train pulls away, and the bus gets quiet again as we head towards town.

A sweet strawberry aroma permeates up to my driver's seat as we proceed down the highway.

As I shake my head, the sweet smell is probably a high school child attempting to vape on the school bus. I will ask our coordinator to check the cameras when I return to the bus lot.

In the meantime, a stern look through the rearview mirror straight into the souls of the students seated in the back of the bus accompanied by, "I don't need to tell you vaping is not permitted on my bus!"

I pull the bus over to the side of the road, set my parking brake, and stand up to address the students.

"I am going to give you one opportunity to give me the vape before I turn you into your principal."

Nobody says a word. Nobody makes a sound.

"Okay, I have given you a chance," I continue. "You are causing everyone on this bus to wait for you to make the right decision!"

A failed attempt once again.

I return to my driver's seat and continue driving to the middle school. What a beautiful morning ruined by a child vaping on the bus.

As we arrive at the middle school, Ms. Payne, a tall, well-dressed Assistant Principal, waves and quickly turns away as she responds to a call on her handheld radio.

Ms. Payne is a kind, well-spoken administrator who clearly loves the children. She stands by my bus and greets every child by their name. She makes every child feel important and acknowledged.

Her kind demeanor makes dropping off the children even more enjoyable, knowing someone welcomes them with pride and devotion.

As my riders get off the school bus, Ms. Payne greets them and offers words of affirmation to every child. She is so joyful, and the children love her.

"Agnus, I adore your sweater today!" she said.

"Good morning, Jamal!" she continued, "I see you brought your science project."

"That's a great way to show everyone our solar system!" she said.

All of my middle school children enter the cafeteria entrance and quickly race inside to have breakfast. The campus serves breakfast to every child and makes sure they all have a good start to their day.

The cafeteria ladies wait for them with everything on display. I often think about sneaking inside for a quick bite to eat, as the breakfast on display looks so delicious!

Pulling out of the middle school, I glance across the campus to see the young football players gathered in groups, going over different tackling techniques. The cross-country coach, Coach Hernandez, is talking with his athletes as they stretch after their morning run.

As I approach the crosswalk, Ms. Felicia, the campus crossing guard, smiles and waves in her reflective jacket. She often brings a speaker to play music and will dance at the intersection.

Gloria is always talking to the students as they cross the street, offering fist bumps to every child and a quick word of encouragement before heading to school.

Turning left onto 4th Street, I head to the high school with my remaining riders. Our town is quite busy in the morning, with everyone headed to work and dropping their kids off at school.

Some folks race across town to grab a cup of coffee to start their day or a box of homemade kolaches, which are an amazing moment of pure deliciousness in the morning!

As we arrive at the enormous monstrosity, commonly referred to as the high school, the remaining students start to gather their belongings, sitting up in their seats.

In Texas, high schools are often the equivalent of small universities. My daughter attended a high school with a comfortable enrollment of over 3,200 students every day.

Everything is bigger in Texas.

Opening the door, the high school children stumble down the steps and turn their frowns upside down to greet their friends in the courtyard outside of the cafeteria.

Our drop-off is actually a social gathering spot for the high school kids before they head inside for class or a quick breakfast.

There are several metal picnic tables and the entire place is a quaint setting for talking to friends or tossing a frisbee back and forth. The smell of fall is in the air, and everyone is looking forward to going to the game on Friday night.

Groups of students gather under the trees and around the tables, talking and laughing or looking at their phones.

All levels of fashion pass through the cafeteria doors. Some children with wet hair and pajama bottoms, and others dressed for success with makeup and stylish clothes. Nostalgic heavy metal t-shirts and ripped jeans are a noticeable trend.

The two assistant principals, Mrs Dillon and Mr Greenwood, watch over the bus drop-off every morning, talking with the students and eagerly waiting for school bell to ring.

Finally, after closing my doors to begin heading to the bus barn, I have to slowly negotiate around the students running across the bus lane like a herd of stray cats.

We quickly stop at the ag barn to drop my last two students. Our agriculture department is amazing. Both students disembark the school bus every morning to feed and care for their animals in preparation for the upcoming county fair in November.

"Have a great day, Julian!" I said.

"Don't forget your water bottle, Stella."

Stella feeds her goat, Vern, every morning. She will show me pictures of her prize goat and explain her efforts to raise her animal and keep him show quality.

Julian is a heavy-set, tall young man who is learning to weld. Julian's father owns a fabrication shop outside of town. His mother is an artist who has several sculptures near the town hall and in Hyde Park.

Julian started raising rabbits this year. He has two rabbits he will show at the county fair. Stella showed off a picture of Julian when he first got his baby rabbits to everyone on the bus. He smiled ear to ear.

Our kids are awesome.

Chapter 4
Sunshine and Rainbows

Returning to the bus barn, I can't wait to run to the bathroom. Since we can't leave kids on our school bus to visit the pearl throne, it is a science and an art to ensure you make it back to the bus barn after your 2-3-hour morning route.

Before coming inside to address nature, I walk around my school bus, checking everything mechanically to ensure I am ready to go this afternoon.

I quickly head to the restroom.

Walking towards the side door, I wave to our dispatcher, Michelle.

"Good morning, Michelle!" I shout.

"I am headed back out to clean my bus."

Waving as I head out the door, Michelle smiles and waves as she picks up the phone with her other hand to answer another call.

As I sweep up an array of debris off the floor of my bus, I find a pink, cellular phone sitting in one of the seats.

Frankly, I am not quite sure how a student can forget their cell phone. You would think their life was dependent on having their cell phone in their possession at all times under normal circumstances.

I guess I need to save another child's social life and turn their beloved cell phone into the dispatch office.

"Have a great day, Michelle!" I said as I dropped the cell phone off to lost and found.

Michelle waves again as she talks on the phone, looks at her computer, and collects bus keys from incoming drivers. She is an amazing, hard-working woman who is really the backbone of our department.

Michelle has been working in the dispatch office for several years. She knows every street, every sub-division, and every apartment complex in our district. She is a wealth of knowledge and experience with a touch of spicy attitude.

"I will take care of this blueberry cake donut, Michelle," I announce as I leave the breakroom with the donut in my grasp.

There's no doubt bus drivers love to eat and socialize.

It takes a special person to drive children to and from school every day.

Most drivers are retired, have prior careers in education, finance, or the military. Others are just raising children and need something to help pay the bills.

The majority of quality bus drivers are patient, trustworthy, and approachable. Honestly, children need to be able to trust in us when they may not have anyone else to confide in during a crisis.

All of our drivers are patient, trustworthy, and approachable; not every bus driver is an old and dusty grump. Besides, we do actually have younger men and women who enjoy the rewards of providing student transportation. We are a melting pot serving kids!

There are actually unspoken benefits to driving a school bus. We do get to see the first day of school for every child we drive to school, and over the years, we get to watch the same children grow up to be young adults and take on the world!

Make no mistake; we are quick to protect our kids and genuinely love them, even the challenging ones. Some of the most dedicated bus drivers you will ever meet are those who transport children with special needs.

Although they transport a smaller number of children, their routes are often longer, and most kids are dropped off at their doorstep at home, so you get to become a part of their extended family.

Harry is a special education driver in our department. Harry has been transporting children on a school bus for over 23 years. He is an older man with gray hair and always wears a cowboy hat. He works with Felicia, a bus monitor or, some would call, a bus attendant. They work every day together and try to accommodate every child with patience and genuine kindness.

Harry picks up a total of 12 children each day and transports them to four different campuses. He has a wheelchair-bound student, several high and low-functioning autistic children, a few behaviorally challenged kids, and a blind child.

Harry drives the school bus around the school district with absolute pride, keeping everyone safe. Harry has never been involved in an accident and has a flawless record as a seasoned bus driver.

He is always on time and has a level of patience like no other driver in our department. In the military, he served in Vietnam and Korea.

Felicia is a kind, soft-spoken woman who is a perfect fit for their school bus. She is gentle and caring throughout the route, situating each child individually, putting on their seat belts, and showing them the attention, they need.

She talks to each child, even if they are non-verbal, letting them know she is there and she cares for each and every one of them. She lets every child know they are important to her.

If you ride along with Harry and Felicia, you will see lots of decorations on their school bus. They have lights, stickers, a box of toys and books, everything a child could want on their school bus and more.

Keeping things consistent and calm fosters the very best environment for their special children. Felicia is masterful at making sure every student is situated and feels welcome on their school bus.

Historically, Harry and Felicia have been working a long time together and have been through a lot. They have witnessed child neglect cases and evidence of physical abuse and they consistently advocate for their children when nobody else will.

Student transportation often includes some significantly dark aspects of education. Unfortunately, not every child has a safe place to go after school.

"It's true!" Harry explained during a special services meeting.

"Bus drivers are the first people to see children in the morning and they are the last to see them before they go home each day!" Harry continued.

"But when things don't seem right, we have to do what is necessary for the safety of our kids!"

"Sometimes, it is not sunshine and rainbows!" He continued, "Seeing a child who has not been bathed in several days or a child who has bruises from abuse is hard!"

"We try to be an angel on their shoulder and find them the help and support they need," Felicia added.

Filing incident reports with Child Protective Services is always difficult for anyone; but, knowing you may be saving a child's life brings relief to everyone involved.

Most families love and care for their children without question. Providing student transportation is undoubtedly a rewarding profession. We have unwavering love for our kids and want the very best for them.

"When we see abuse or neglect," Felicia commented,

"We are legally bound to report it to the authorities." she continued.

"Some families think we do it because we don't like them.", she said, "That is simply not true!"

"Our children do not choose where they live. They do not choose how they are taken care of each day," Harry explained.

"They cannot control whether they have food to eat or a clean bed to sleep in each night." He said, "Some children wear the same clothes several days in a row!"

"We have children who have holes in their shoes, no belt to hold up their pants." Felicia added, "Last year, we had a child who didn't even have running water or any electricity in her home for weeks."

As we transport children, we see the very best our parents, grandparents, and caregivers can send to school. They do their best to provide food, clothing, and other necessities for their children.

Some parents are so poor that just cannot make ends meet without some assistance. Raising children is hard and can be very expensive.

Over the years, our bus drivers see families struggling and suffering each day and want to do more. They may pick up a pair of new shoes for a child, bring protein bars and bottles of water to give to their kids who may need a little extra energy getting their school day off to a good start.

Everybody works together to give our kids the best chance to succeed.

Chapter 5
Turkey and Stuffing

Last year, I met a remarkable woman who drove a school bus for a neighboring school district. Her name was Francis Stone.

Over the course of an entire school year, Francis watched a young teenage boy get on and off the school bus every day. Francis got to know him really well because he rode the school bus longer than any other child.

It didn't take long to realize Charlie absolutely needed to go to school every day. Charlie didn't need to go to school just to learn mathematics and social studies. He needed to go to school so he would have food to eat.

Charlie was a skinny young man who lived in a singlewide mobile home in a field at the edge of the county. When Charlie was home, he often sat alone as his recently divorced father worked odd jobs for peanuts and came home to drink beer and watch television.

Francis watched Charlie come out of his mobile home every day and run towards the school bus. Charlie struggled to carry his things; but, his face always lit up when he saw Ms. Francis.

"Good morning, Charlie!"

"Morning, Ms. Francis!" Charlie enthusiastically responded.

Since Charlie was the first student she picked up every morning, she would often talk with him one-on-one for a short time before the next bus stop, sometimes longer.

One day, Charlie explained that his father drinks a lot and there is never anything to eat at home. Francis started bringing snacks she would give Charlie to get him going.

As the holidays approached, Francis got a great idea to purchase a Thanksgiving turkey and all the fixings to give to Charlie to take home!

Francis was so excited to help him and looked forward to see the smile on his face. After her morning route, Francis went to the local grocery store and bought a ten-pound turkey, a box of instant stuffing, a bag of white potatoes, and a few other things. As she checked out, she quickly grabbed a pumpkin pie for dessert.

Francis couldn't wait to give everything to Charlie and his father to enjoy over Thanksgiving. After afternoon dismissal, Charlie stepped on the school bus.

Francis eagerly waited to give him the Thanksgiving dinner groceries at the end of her route. She waited so as to not embarrass him in front of his friends. She was so excited!

Afterall, she would drop him off last so there would be ample opportunity for the dialog and presentation.

As Charlie's bus stop arrived, she said, "Charlie, I have a gift for you for Thanksgiving!"

Charlie smiled and couldn't believe his eyes. Two days to Thanksgiving, Charlie had more food than he had seen in the past few weeks in the three grocery bags she handed him.

Francis couldn't wait to see how her gift would change Charlie's upcoming holiday. She knew he was worth the effort and that they were struggling financially. She believed the father and son could enjoy some quality time together through her efforts.

The next day, Francis honked the horn anxiously waiting for Charlie to step outside. The door swung open and Charlie slowly walked to the bus, head drawn downward. As he stepped onto the bus, Francis was horrified. Her eyes immediately welled up with tears.

Charlie had a cut over his right eye and a large bruise on his cheek. His bottom lip was swollen and he dropped his head as he came up the stairwell.

Francis closed the doors and drove a mile or two before she pulled the bus over and turned around to speak to Charlie.

"What happened, Charlie?"

After racing into the house and placing the groceries on the kitchen table, Charlie anxiously awaited his father to come home from work. Charlie happily presented the groceries to his father explaining how kind the bus driver was to have bought them all of the groceries for their Thanksgiving holiday.

His father immediately became enraged. He berated Charlie for sharing their financial situation with others and slammed the frozen Turkey into the trash can. Charlie tried to defend the gesture by explaining himself.

His failed attempt resulted in two strikes to his face and being shoved into the kitchen table. Charlie slid across the top of the kitchen table, knocked over the chair, and slammed into the hardwood floor, hitting his head and right shoulder.

His father swept the remaining items off the table with his arm and across the kitchen. Cursing, his father ordered Charlie to go to his room.

Charlie ran to his room weeping and locked his bedroom door.

As Charlie hid in his closet, his father sat on the recliner, eating the pumpkin pie with a spoon, flipping through the channels on the television.

Francis was devastated and ended up eventually quitting driving a school bus shortly after the incident. She was heartbroken and blamed herself for what happened to Charlie.

"Sometimes we can't help!" she exclaimed. "Maybe I shouldn't do this anymore!"

Francis resigned over the Thanksgiving break.

Her entire department was sad to see Francis leave. Her director personally filed the Child Protective Services report against the father for his abuse and neglect.

"You are always welcome here!" the Director told Francis before she left.

"We will miss you so much, Francis!" the Coordinator added, "You did the right thing!" The coordinator shook her head with tears in her eyes.

Our coordinator, Emily Paige, maintains our entire transportation department that supports countless routes and over sixty employees. Emily has developed close relationships with just about every driver the school district employs.

She can tell you professional details about each driver, monitor, and staff member in intimate detail after working with most of them for the past several years.

Emily has been around transportation for the past 16 years and she has developed an impressive resume that includes institutional learning and her attendance to countless training conferences. She has held every position in student transportation except the transportation director role.

Emily certainly will take over the transportation department after our current Director leaves or moves up to Assistant Superintendent. She is amazing!

Emily is married, has three children, all grown, and enjoys crafting in her spare time. Emily never attended college; however, she is masterful at her profession.

She started a family early in her life and fell into driving school buses for extra money. Now, she leads an entire department of bus drivers and is truly the glue that keeps everyone stuck together.

Chapter 6
Pit Crew

After eating lunch and getting my oil changed on my pickup truck, I headed down to the feed store to grab some deer corn. We enjoy watching the deer in the evening, catching a quick snack before bedding down for the night.

While shopping, I ran into a parent of one of the children I transport. Smiling as she passes, Ms. Phillips offers a kind gesture of allowing me to check out before her. Ms. Phillips has two children, one elementary student and a toddler. She appears to be expecting a third child by the looks of her standing in line.

I thank her and pay for my things before departing. Living in the community you support is always rewarding, provided you are good at what you do.

As my afternoon route time approaches, I head to the bus barn. Grabbing my keys from the dispatch office and the paperwork for a newly enrolled student, I quickly walk to my school bus. I grab my tire knocker and begin inspecting my school bus for any mechanical issues once again. My assigned school bus is a really good and dependable bus to drive. Our mechanics work hard to take care of all of our buses. They keep us rolling!

Gabriel is finishing his pre-inspection and shouts across his hood, "I'll bet I beat you back tonight!"

He loves the competition even though our routes are not even at all. I nod and smile knowing I will beat him to the yard.

He will still be dropping the children off when I am home and relaxing from the day.

Gabriel is married to a retired school principal. The man is always happy, joking around, and willing to help anyone. His children are all grown, and he enjoys spending time with his wife during his mid-day breaks. He knows he has to drive a school bus because his wife will never let him sit around at home. They are both foodies and love to check out different restaurants.

Gabriel provides our department with dry humor and puts on his "serious" hat to lead the training section. He has a wealth of knowledge and experience.

After finishing inspecting my school bus, I stopped in to see the mechanics.

"Afternoon, boys!" I shout.

"How has your day been going?" I added.

They both smile and continue working. They aren't the most sociable fellas.

Robert Russell, our lead mechanic, has been working on school buses most of his life. When he was younger, he worked on race cars, changing transmissions in the pits.

When he got older, Robert left racing to work at a school bus dealership. Eventually, he realized supporting a fleet of school buses for a school district was something he enjoyed more than working in a dealership setting.

Bobby Ray Cox, a full-time mechanic and part-time bus driver, works alongside Robert. They are like two old women, arguing over nothing and harassing each other while keeping our school bus fleet afloat.

Bobby Ray is a big guy, significantly overweight. He enjoys turning wrenches and showing his pride for his favorite college football team. You see, Bobby Ray is a University of Texas Longhorn fan. He drives a golf cart around every day and takes care of the fluids on every bus.

The man is proud of his Longhorn decorations.

One day, Robert decided he would get one over on Bobby Ray. He went out and purchased an array of Texas Christian University decorations and went wild on Bobby Ray's golf cart. What a sight to see!

As Robert drove the golf cart out to Bobby Ray working on a school bus in our east lot, he proudly got off the golf cart and didn't even look back to see Bobby Ray horrified.

Robert made sure the golf cart was inundated with purple decorations and TCU Horned Frog garb. Hilarious!

Stanley is the mechanic's helper on staff. His official position is as a special education bus driver; however, he spent most of his life as a mechanic.

Stanley is a bit too old to be turning wrenches, but he enjoys doing little things around the shop. He will help fuel buses, fix torn seats, change lights, and do oil changes. He is not a fan of doing big jobs anymore; that ship has sailed.

Stanley was in tears, laughing at the purple atrocity rolling across the bus lot. He knew Bobby Ray was devastated, and he couldn't wait to see how Bobby Ray would respond in kind. To no avail, Bobby shed grown man crocodile tears.

Firing up my school bus, I settle into my seat and roll my shoulders back to prepare for the afternoon. As I get ready, several buses have already headed out on their afternoon route and I will be headed the same way very soon.

Looking across the bus lot, I see our coordinator and our director walking the yard, talking amongst themselves and waving to the drivers as they leave for the afternoon. Just before I leave the gate, I pause to let a fuel truck pull in to fill our underground tanks.

The sun is blazing and I have my air conditioning working overtime.

Jessica, an elementary bus driver, seems to be delayed as a mechanic looks under her hood and talks with her. Jessica tends to find something wrong with her school bus quite often.

Sometimes, I think she doesn't want to drive and finds things to delay her route.

Our mechanics are as old as the hills, so it's not that she wants to spend time in the shop all goo-goo-eyed.

I think she just worries too much. We often wonder if she is as concerned with her own personal vehicle as she is frequently turning in work order after work order for her school bus.

You would think the school district bought her bus from a junkyard, according to the frequency of mechanical discrepancies she finds within any given week.

Chapter 7
Dismissal Mafia

I head to my first campus and pull in behind three other school buses already staged in the bus lane. The parents have already started lining up over an hour ago to be the first to pick up their children.

It seems a bit odd that folks wait up to an hour and a half to pick up their child first versus waiting in line.

Walking alongside the countless vehicles, it may be a place they enjoy themselves. The school resource officer glances into each car as he heads to the gate to open it for dismissal. Some parents are sleeping; others are on their cell phones. Little ones jumping around in the back seats, a mom listening to the radio quietly. A father nodding off to the sound of classical music.

You can see the school resource officer placing traffic cones. Here comes a dad who evidently got sent at the last minute, to pick up the kids, by his wife, who normally picks up the children and understands how everything works on the elementary school.

Today, Mom is at a doctor's appointment, and Dad is violating the sacred rules of dismissal driving laws enforced by the United Nations and the Federal Government.

As he tries to cut off another vehicle, the "dismissal mafia" are quick to cuss him out and validate his incompetence with their horns.

God forbid the man doesn't follow the rules he is clearly unaware of to meet the expectations of his spouse. The devil himself wouldn't violate the traffic patterns of an elementary school campus.

"What was he thinking?"

"Who does he think he is…seriously!"

As we secure our buses and patiently wait for dismissal, the drivers gather to have a quick discussion before the kids are released.

Samantha, a new bus driver, asks how to get her air conditioning to work a little better. A fellow driver explains to her that in the Texas heat, you can only hope for moderate air conditioning.

"School buses aren't made to overcome 105 degrees of Texas heat!" she mumbles.

Finally, the children start coming out to the school bus. Inside the building, there are two ladies calling their names, putting on their backpacks, and sending them out by bus number.

Another lady stands midway down the sidewalk to keep the children from running to the school bus, falling, and knocking out their beautiful, new, front teeth. She seems to be patient and kind to the children.

As the students step onto the school bus, they look exhausted. A few children have hats they have made in their classroom. Others are carrying colored pictures and worksheets. Colored to perfection, they are proud of their little hats.

I walk down the aisle to help my littles get into their booster seats and put their seat belts on before we leave.

"I dropped my pack pack," a preschool child says as they are being buckled into their booster seat.

"Here you go!" I respond.

Some children quickly fall asleep before I even leave campus, and others are wound up for sound. Our littles are all placed in booster seats to keep them safe throughout our route. We try to avoid our littles from flying out of their seats when an inexperienced driver cuts us off or slams on their brakes just before a yellow light.

Our littles are our precious commodity. What is a little, you say? Our littles are preschool, kindergarten, and first-grade students who are too little, too cute, and too ornery.

Most of our drivers are delighted to get just a few little on their school bus. They are so inquisitive and see things in its purest sense.

For those who don't prefer littles on their school bus, they often have to be reminded that children at this age do not understand sarcasm. They do not respond to a dry sense of humor. More importantly, littles need and want more than most children, and you have to be patient with them.

"Can I get some hanitizer?" a child asked.

"What?" a substitute bus driver asked.

"Hanitizer…" she asked, "for my hands!"

"Oh! You need hand sanitizer." the bus driver giggled.

"Sure!"

The bus driver pumped some hand sanitizer into the child's little hands and she rubbed her hands together with determination.

"Thank you!"

"You're very welcome, Kelsey!"

Our school district policy requires our parents to meet the school bus each day to pick up their littles at the bus stop before and after school. We do this to ensure our kids get home safe and to stay on time throughout our route. It's funny how easily one late parent can turn an entire route into chaos timewise.

After a recent child abduction in a neighboring community, everyone takes every possible precaution to ensure our children are safe to and from school. We all have zero tolerance for strangers near our bus stops.

Make no mistake, every bus driver believes every student is priceless; but, we try to give extra support to those children who are too little to realize they are at risk of injury or death moving around a school bus.

"We want them to believe riding the school bus is a magical experience!" Christina explained as she smiled and nodded her head.

"Our young children look at riding our school bus as an adventure, especially when we are permitted to dress up and decorate our school bus to a theme."

Last year, we all dressed up as superheroes for our children. The elementary school bus drivers love when we dress up because the children listen as we try to spark their imagination.

"Are you really a superhero, Mr. Bus Driver?" a child asked.

"Yes…in my spare time, Michael," I responded.

"What is your superpower, Mr. Bus Driver?" another child inquired.

"I can talk to animals," I explained. "I can talk to cats, dogs, chickens, and even bees."

"What do the chickens talk about?" a little girl said.

"Well, the chickens I talk to seem to ask me for more food," I responded. "They are always hungry!"

We continued talking throughout the route as I explained my conversations with the animals around our ranch.

I try my best to keep the stories interesting but still truthful. I never told the kids the animals don't talk back. How much fun would that be?

Lynn is a seasoned bus driver our Director hired last year to drive our littles. She is a kind-hearted, punctual professional who clearly cares about her students. Picking a person to transport all preschool and kindergarten children can certainly be tricky. It takes a very, special person with genuine kindness and lots of patience.

Our littles can be mischievous, grumpy, happy, sad, or all of the above during a typical route. Multiplying those demeanors by the number of children riding on one school bus, and you get… a rolling circus!

Ms. Lynn is masterful at addressing every student's needs, as she is equally talented in parent communication and keeping focused on safety. Ms. Lynn contacts and collaborates with parents and caregivers for pick up and drop off daily. She skillfully adjusts her pickups and drop offs and still gets her littles to school on time.

It certainly takes a special human being to do what Ms. Lynn does with style and grace!

Chapter 8
Running Reds

Everyone is on board and we are headed to my second elementary campus. The afternoon is starting out smooth as silk. Everyone is belted into their seats. Older children are seated and looking at their electronic devices, and the Assistant Principal is waving us on like a Formula One race.

Mr. Stanley looks tired. I can only imagine how long his days must feel to him.

We leave Manor Elementary and head to Alexander Elementary. As we leave campus, I glance to the right to see countless parents lined up at the main entrance of the elementary school.

Picking up their students and walking them to their parked cars, the parents appear joyful and full of energy in learning what their children did in school throughout the day.

Children are carrying art projects and lunch boxes, backpacks and toys, and don't forget whatever they brought for show and tell.

Dads are all smiles picking up their sons and daughters which may be a treat from the norm. Construction trailers attached to obnoxiously large pickup trucks, dads are tossing their children into the back seat and pulling off with big billows of smoke from their loud diesel engines.

One mom looks like she is leading a flock, as she extends her arms to gather her children. A teacher's aide told us she has eight children, five of them attend their elementary school.

"It takes a special couple to raise eight children!" I think.

My wife and I raised four ourselves and how chaotic our lives became in such a short period of time.

As we drive by the School Resource Officer, he waves and smiles as the children exclaim, "There is Officer Ramos!"

Several riders look through their windows to wave back at him. Dismissal activities continue as we drive down Florence Avenue heading out.

Turning the corner, I look into my rearview mirror, and I can see Adam, our kindergartener, has found his way out of his booster seat.

He is running back and forth, up and down the aisle. His sister Anna looks up when I called her name.

"Anna..." I ask. "Can you please ask Adam to sit with you?"

"Yes, Sir!" she responds.

She kindly asks her brother to sit with her, and she opens a book she had finds in his backpack to show him the pictures as she reads it to him.

As I pull to the side of the road, Anna stands up and walks Adam to his seat. I guide Adam back into his booster, secure his seat belt, and hand him his action figure off the floor. Adam begins to play with his toy and we are off to the races.

Adam smiles as he looks out the window, showing his superhero the cows outside.

"Thank you so much, Anna!"

"You're welcome!" she says as she smiles.

As I turn onto Oak Street, I can faintly hear a child sobbing somewhere on the school bus. At the next stop light, I hit the noise button, and then I knew somebody was crying.

I peer through the mirror and ask the students.

"Who is crying?"

"Victor!" the children reply.

"What's wrong?" I ask.

"He dropped his apple on the floor, and it rolled up to the front of the bus!" Sophia says.

Sophia Rosales, Cynthia's older sister, is in second grade. She loves to inform anyone of anything they might need to hear.

She will tell you loud and proud before anyone else can possibly respond. Sophia is extremely extroverted and enjoys talking about anything. Sophia might be a news anchor or a reporter in the future, who knows?

As a neighboring student consoles Victor and he stops crying, I am coming to the painful realization that his apple is lost or at least not fit for human consumption.

Nobody mentions to Victor he was not allowed to eat on the school bus; most consider his loss its own consequence.

Unfortunately, dirt, crayon fragments, and an eyelash are permanently attached to Victor's apple. We will not be introducing the apple back to our friend, Victor, anytime soon.

We continue down 3rd Avenue and stop at another red light. Our town is inundated with red lights. You would figure members of our community would be accustomed to stopping at red lights; however, more times than not, they drive right past my flashing red lights when I am loading or unloading children all the time.

In most communities, if you don't know when a school bus turns on its "reds" and the little stop sign comes out, that means "STOP!"

Every bus driver's heart stops when someone runs their "reds" and places a child in danger. It is pure ignorance and it is punishable by a hefty fine.

Sometimes, things just have a way of taking care of themselves. Our director was recently greeted by a Game Warden. Game Wardens are always driving around our county to keep the wildlife under control and enforce the laws.

If you are unaware, a game warden has quite a bit of authority. From checking your freezers for poached game to issuing a traffic citation for wrongdoing, these folks have almost unlimited authority.

One day a game warden, Officer John Wilkerson, had witnessed a vehicle driven by an obnoxious driver pass my "reds" just outside of the middle school. The driver veered off the road and made a valiant effort to not hit the big, red stop signs sticking out in his path.

Coming to the rescue, Officer Wilkerson pulled the driver over and issued a hefty ticket. Of course, the driver decided to appear in court to fight the citation and was trying to circumvent taking responsibility for his own carelessness.

Ironically, the game warden had dropped by the transportation department and met with my Director, who provided the school bus video surveillance footage necessary to substantiate the citation.

"Case <u>not</u> dismissed, Sir!"

Chapter 9
Big Yellow School Bus

Training to drive a school bus, we learn as bus drivers that our buses can withstand most vehicle collisions. An average school bus actually weighs 16 tons empty. From small compact cars to goofy, jacked-up pickup trucks with funny lights underneath them, the steel frame of a school bus withstands most collisions according to physics.

Drivers on their cell phones or distracted drivers seem to be running into school buses in our district more often than not. Earlier this year, we had a lady drive right into the side of our school bus while it was at a complete stop. Her vehicle was totaled and our school bus had a tiny scratch.

According to her husband, his wife was a new driver and allegedly stepped on the gas pedal instead of the brake and hit our bus.

Accidents happen every day; school buses make the news quicker than most vehicle accidents by a long shot.

People are more judgmental when a school bus is involved because they almost always consider their own children being on the school bus.

Even the police and firemen get irritated when someone hits our school buses.

During our latest distracted driver slamming into the back of our school bus, the first responders had a roasting at the accident scene.

"Just be patient, Mr. Cellphone. The DPS Officer will issue you a ticket!" a paramedic said.

"Don't you worry, kind Sir, he or she will reward you for your stupidity!" a fireman joked as he swept up the plastic debris from the vehicle.

"Stupid!" a bystander said as he shook his head. "Just plain stupid!"

The accident with the distracted driver resulted in over $15,000 in damages and two students being transported to the hospital. The school bus driver who was also injured, regardless of fault, will be subjected to a drug screening, have an accident on their driving record with the Federal Motor Carrier Safety Administration, and be restricted from driving until the video surveillance, police investigation, and district safety review are completed.

"I am so sorry!" the distracted driver exclaimed as the bus driver was wheeled towards the ambulance.

"I safely transport children every day without my phone, Sir." He grimaced and tried to shout. "The least you could do is stay off your phone and pay attention!"

Most first responders who heard our bus driver smiled and nodded in approval.

He was absolutely right!

When a new bus driver gets their license, they really haven't driven a school bus. Even though they may have driven a tractor trailer, driving a school bus is so much different. Rolling down the highway and hauling a trailer full of dog food does not compare to driving 45 children headed home after a long day at school.

Do you know how children can affect the overall ability of a human being to perform regular tasks?

It can best be assessed by you standing in a grocery line with two items while a child screams from the shopping cart for the candy they have been refused. Add two more children are slap-fighting in the next aisle and another child is telling her mother what's happening repeatedly while the Mom ignores them all.

We can add a price check on aisle seven to make things worse if you like.

Now, drive a large vehicle in a sea of distracted drivers and make absolutely no mistakes. Don't lose your cool, and you might become a bus driver. Whatever you do, don't scream or holler at the kids either!

If this interests you, let us address the second critical factor to becoming a professional bus driver. Understanding children and how you can get them to do what they don't want to do willingly takes a lifetime in itself.

If you claim to still be cool as a cucumber, let us address the second determining factor to becoming a school bus driver. You must be able to understand the children themselves.

Let's start with our little children, mostly kindergarteners and preschool-aged children. These children are ninja masters at are capable of escape and deception. They have a keen ability to get out of their seat belts, slide down the seat to the bus floor, and appear anywhere at any given moment.

Now, let's mix in some middle school students; typically, sixth-grade students will fit the requirement. These students offer a distinct aroma like no other. You see, deodorant is only used by some. Aerosol deodorant and cheap perfume and colognes for others. A "less is more" option has not been implemented in their lives to date. Some days, they make your eyes water.

Sprinkle in some high school freshmen or eighth graders. These individuals, depending on their maturity level, can aggravate or annoy anyone within a mile radius. They are skillful manipulators and they will attempt to arbitrate every bus rule they do not agree to follow.

Finally, let's consider adding some seasoned high school students. Now, high school students can effectively assume two different roles on your school bus.

Either they are sweet, supportive, stewards of the rules and provide additional supervision of the younger children; or, they are obnoxious, sometimes verbally abusive, children who have adopted an additional foreign language of profanity. A language derived from social media, smart phone applications, and profane music lyrics.

Periodically, verbal and physical conflicts occur on our school buses, and we try to stop them by offering "on-the-spot" corrections. Following up with words of affirmation once they comply to our requests or re-direction can also help.

Our sixth-grade boys and eighth-grade girls have an extremely difficult time following directions.

Chemically, understanding and exercising reasonable thought when hormones are governing the situation can prove to be difficult.

EMERGENCY DOOR

IT IS IN VIOLATION OF STATE LAW
AND STATE BOARD POLICY
FOR UNAUTHORIZED PERSONNEL
TO BOARD THIS VEHICLE
(VIOLATORS WILL BE PROSECUTED)

1469

Chapter 10
Conflict Resolution

A few months ago, two middle school girls had a pretty significant conflict between themselves on a school bus. In education, you learn that different age groups and genders foster very different behaviors. Adjusting to hormone overload is a real thing!

On this particular day, the two middle school girls' conflict started with a verbal confrontation that escalated into text messages, then social media posts, and eventually, family members arriving at a school bus during the afternoon route to try to support their children in the conflict.

Sometimes, we need to let kids be kids. After all, playground rules always apply in these situations.

On a desolate country road, Helen James, who genuinely sees very little drama on her school bus, found herself trying to calm down two middle school girls before they physically fought each other.

As the conflict ensued, wouldn't you know arguing turned into name calling, threats followed, and both children began texting their families for support. Social media makes things so much worse in a situation like this particular incident.

As their conflict escalated, the bus driver pulled over to call the dispatch office for assistance. The bus was located along the side of the road beside a large pasture.

Before anyone arrived from the school district to help the bus driver, the two angry family members arrived onsite.

Using cell phone technology, along with global positioning, the angry family members quickly found the school bus.

Upon arrival, the two angry adults began threatening the school bus driver and actually tried to open the school bus doors to board the school bus. The bus driver immediately called the dispatch office again on the two-way radio and pleaded for assistance.

Since the school bus doors were closed with an air lock system, the bus driver felt safe enough to head to the middle of the school bus to try to settle the conflict between the two middle school children.

As if things couldn't have gotten any worse, a child sitting in the front passenger side seat, who attended the safety assembly in the beginning of the school year, hit the emergency release button on the secured bus doors, releasing them, and providing the two angry family members an opportunity to board the school bus.

After realizing the angry family members had boarded the bus, Helen quickly tried to block the two from getting to the children until she was physically shoved out of the way.

"No!" Helen screamed. "You're not allowed on this bus!"

"Get off of my bus!" Helen boldly said.

After shoving her way past Helen and reaching the middle school child, one of the adults began striking the child with her fists as she pulled the student out of her seat. The second adult joined the assault as they both slammed the middle school child onto the floor.

Then, the two angry family members turned to the older freshman sister sitting across the aisle and began to punch her repeatedly.

Both children sustained concussions and multiple bruises from the incident. Thankfully, the entire incident was captured on camera.

"Don't forget, ladies, cameras don't lie!"

The district official and the local authorities arrived shortly after the two family members got off the school bus. The damage was done.

Eventually, the two adults were arrested and prosecuted, serving two months in jail after receiving felony convictions. According to our safety procedures, Helen pulled the school bus over and tried to resolve the issue.

Stopping the fight and separating the children, Helen would have safely returned to campus and met with the school resource officers to address the physical conflict.

In our opinion, Helen was an absolute hero!

She stood between two angry adults and her children and attempted to defend them. She continued to aggressively get the two women off the school bus to protect her students.

Helen kept her children calm throughout the entire incident, followed safety procedures, and after the incident, transported every remaining student home safely.

We were so proud of Helen.

She was recognized in our department meeting and the district school board recognized her as well.

We learned the details of the incident from our Director during a monthly safety meeting. Protecting children and understanding the potential of unauthorized individuals boarding your school bus is a risk we all have to consider.

We couldn't help but be proud of our fellow bus driver. She did everything she could to protect her kids despite extremely hostile circumstances.

Helen was never the same after the incident.

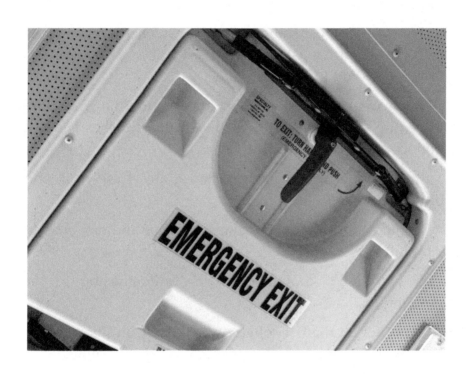

Chapter 11
Morning Meetings

Our department safety meetings are pretty enjoyable. Although our Director talks and talks until our ears bleed, we have a chance to all be together.

We do get to eat some really great food throughout the meeting. As previously mentioned, I did say, "Bus drivers love to eat, didn't I?"

A few weeks ago, we met right after our morning route and the entire department brought in breakfast dishes laid out potluck style across two long tables.

Breakfast casseroles, biscuits and gravy, fresh fruit, and bacon. Lots of bacon!

Donuts and kolaches, breakfast burritos and empanadas. Absolutely delicious!

If you don't know, empanadas are amazing in the morning!

Don't forget the hot coffee, an array of fruit juices, and a hot apple cider made with cinnamon. What a morning!

After eating myself into a food coma, listening to the Director was next to impossible. I was nodding off like a kid at a headbanger's ball, drooling occasionally.

Remember when I mentioned bus drivers are grandmas, grandpas, military veterans, and parents? Let me tell you, bus drivers whip up great, home-cooked dishes for everyone to eat with little or no notice. Some are health conscious, and others are not health conscious at all. I appreciate the latter of the two myself.

Sugar and sweets and lots to eat, that's the way we love to meet!

As the meeting begins, everyone noshes on their selections from a delectable breakfast buffet that will rival any restaurant or diner.

Our leaders recognize accomplishments, provide safety reminders, and discuss different scenarios we can encounter on our school bus. Our coordinator often takes time to explain specific scenarios and answer questions our drivers ask since she has so much experience.

Everyone is present including our mechanics. Almost every meeting, we do something fun with our "wedding planner", who normally serves as our field trip coordinator and afternoon dispatcher. Gloria is a creative, kind and extremely sociable member of our transportation office staff. She works hard to keep our daily routine interesting by coming up with different activities we can do on and off our school bus.

From tropical grass skirts to sports jerseys, our drivers dress up for the kids and receive tickets for prizes at our monthly department meetings from Gloria.

Winning a raffle at any department meeting is the bee's knees! The prizes could be candy, gift cards or something else really cool.

Now, receiving the "stinky sock" award for the dirtiest bus is not very fun, and I assume it is certainly frowned upon to drive a dirty bus anyway?

Gloria enjoys seeing the smiles on bus drivers' faces and they adore her and her efforts to help boost morale and our department culture.

Drivers will wear ridiculous outfits, spend their own money on treats for their children, and decorate their bus simply because they know the children love it. Sometimes, they can be competitive; therefore, tickets are included to keep things interesting.

Chapter 12
Channel 4

Listening to the two-way radio, you need to sit down and hold on to your britches.

"Oh Lord, our people love talking on the radio!"

We genuinely try our best to keep it professional. We honestly do…but sometimes we need to make a joke, slide a comment, or correct another driver.

It's in our blood to say something when nobody else will. We cannot lay on our horns or use profane language. We do our best to represent our school district. We cannot forget that we are entrusted by parents, grandparents, and our entire community to do what is right without question. Of course, traffic and distracted drivers can make our efforts difficult.

We do try our best. Then, there are those who just can't help it. A quick two-way radio transmission. A short comment about something trivial and we our off to the races!

Some bus drivers watched too much seventies television in their childhood and wholeheartedly believe the two-way radio is their personal venue for comedy relief.

When things are running smoothly, the radio becomes a playing field for everyone. Several months ago, a few drivers were intrigued by a driver who routinely transmitted in poor English. The man misinterpreted 10-4 for the phrase "Channel 4". As soon as everyone confirmed what he was actually saying, it was game on!

For months, we played around with ending our radio transmissions with a subtle "Channel 4" acknowledgment.

You would think he would have been offended. But, the man continued to utilize his misinterpreted phrase without fail.

As he settled into our family, the drivers looked forward to him coming on the radio, wishing everyone a "Good Morning!" and he would always finish his greeting with "God Bless America!"

We do honestly try to limit radio traffic on the radio by shifting over to another channel for some side dialog; however, who can really listen to our thoughts?

Unfortunately, there are drivers who have no idea about this practice because they think the entire transportation department genuinely cares about the school bus driver in front of them who still has their turn signal on or their flashing red lights and stop sign. Goodness gracious!

We are an inquisitive bunch though. Bus drivers are socially dependent for the most part. After all, when we do not have kids, we get bored.

Remember, I mentioned the other channel on the radio. Well, let me tell ya! Switching over to listen to a little bit of gossip never hurt anyone! It is like a soap opera sometimes!

"I can't believe he didn't let me drive past him!"

"Hey, Route 13, turn your reds off on campus!" another complained.

"Did you hear what she said about him?"

"Yes, can you believe it?"

We do like gossip even though we say we don't. Driving a school bus full of students tends to give us the opportunity every once in a while to act like children ourselves.

I am not insulting bus drivers, I just believe we need some interaction when we drive the same routes over and over again. Adult conversation accompanied by a little stress relief and comedy is a recipe for success!

Let's face it, conversations with our students are limited to "Sit down!", "Put that away!" or "Stop hitting him!".

"Jeffrey, don't make me come back there!"

Very rarely can we say what we are thinking because it may include profane language or vile threats.

So, we rewind before we get in trouble...

"Jeffrey, young man. Could you please sit on your bottom so you can stay safe all the way home?"

After Jeffrey finally sits down, "Thank you so much, Jeffrey. You are the best!"

It is all in the presentation.

Chapter 13
Cameras and Videos

I am really not sure how many times a human being needs to remind a child to do something. The other day, I was at the grocery store between routes. I watched a middle-aged mother tell a child to sit down in the grocery cart fourteen times before she finally "sat" him down.

Fourteen times!

Some would say she was being verbally or physically abusive.

When I was growing up, "sitting" him down was accompanied with a "whopping".

Not anymore, folks!

In this situation, a young lady at the cash register looked at the mom like she did something wrong and all the mother was trying to do was buy some groceries without any drama.

You would think it would be acceptable to discipline your child after requesting him or her to sit down fourteen times in public with no response.

Judgmental people can make student transportation extremely difficult as well.

First, bus drivers cannot discipline children, raise their voices, or even stop the school bus without triggering a string of complaints on social media. Not to mention, our dispatch office would be flooded with nasty phone calls, including at least one request for someone to be fired, reprimanded, or both.

Back in the day, a bus driver yelling at kids was a normal occurrence. Seasoned school bus drivers would brake check their kids every time they refused to sit down in their seats and smile when they did it.

Today, school districts don't condone brake checking anyone; however, rest assured...we are all wishing we could! Unfortunately, our students smartphones or the security cameras on the bus would catch us red-handed; so, no unauthorized or inappropriate behavior folks.

Usually, our students do not even ask permission to take pictures or videos on their smart phones. Fights, arguments, and other incidents are commonly caught by multiple students without fail. What is more concerning is when they immediately post the video or the photo online without asking anyone or taking responsibility for anything that results from posting it online.

I keep telling myself cameras and videos are actually good. If we are doing what is right all the time, even when nobody is looking, we shouldn't have anything to worry about as bus drivers. Right?

If we do what is right, even when nobody else is looking, we are good, I believe.

I do find it intriguing that students are being held accountable for their actions by their peers. Upstanding students are turning in videos and pictures to their campuses of adverse behavior they witness.

Our students are reporting students vaping, assaults, harassment, bullying, inappropriate language and other behaviors normally missed by adults. Honestly, our students are strong and willing to advocate for others.

As bus drivers, we submit reports to the transportation office, we provide the actual time an incident occurs, and the transportation coordinator will review the camera footage to determine the validity of our claim.

After our coordinator finds an incident on video, she sends the footage to the campus administrators to generate a discipline referral. Then, the student has to meet with their assistant principal an explain their actions. It is actually pretty efficient, it just takes a while.

Ladies and gentlemen, there is always comedy in reviewing video surveillance. Once in a while, a driver forgets they are on camera and can be seen on camera surveillance singing at the top of their lungs to music when the bus is empty.

Forget karaoke. We are talking about celebrity status!

Our coordinator absolutely loves to watch footage of our bus drivers preparing for the local talent show or the next reality singing competition on video. The majority of bus drivers include choreography, especially when they are grooving to their favorite song.

Genuinely, everyone is thankful for the camera surveillance because it protects our drivers from malicious accusations that put their employment at risk.

More often than not, our young riders who may receive a disciplinary report for their behavior will make extremely convincing accusations about their bus driver. Thank goodness these accusations are dismissed upon review of the camera surveillance footage.

Over the years, our cameras have caught vehicle accidents, student fights, parents attempting to come on our school buses, and drivers talking on their cell phones or yelling at children.

Cameras have also verified genuine kindness, children helping others, bus drivers defending their riders against a threat, and many other unbelievable acts of selfless service.

Cameras keep everyone safe.

Chapter 14
Staying Calm

Patrick Williams, a young man who joined our school district driving school buses three years ago, was caught on camera just recently. Patrick was about to drop off his children in a large apartment complex when he saw a child having a major seizure in the aisle of his school bus.

Patrick secured his bus less than a football field away from the apartment complex and headed back to check on the child. He quickly returned to the radio to ask dispatch for help.

"Dispatch, I am going to need some help, please!" he said on the two-way radio. "I have a child who is going to need an ambulance!"

"Please contact 911. I am located in the movie theater parking lot!" Patrick quickly transmitted to the dispatcher monitoring the radio. "The student is having a seizure!"

After asking for help, Patrick called his Director on his cell phone and within minutes, the Director showed up beside the school bus.

Trained to provide first aid, Patrick addressed the children, and the Director began assessing the young female student, who was now unconscious.

"Do not allow anyone on the school bus except emergency services!" the Director exclaimed.

Receiving text messages from their students on the school bus, numerous parents from the apartment complex came running towards the school bus parked in the movie theater parking lot.

As the authorities began to arrive, the local police came to the school bus doors.

"A police officer is asking what you want him to do?" Patrick inquired.

"Please ask him to keep the parents from entering the school bus. I will address them when the paramedics get here!" he said.

"If the police can handle the parents, you can focus on the rest of our children on the bus." he responded.

Patrick watched the police officer immediately address the parents who lived in the apartment complex who eagerly wanted their children off the school bus. He calmly addressed the crowd of concerned parents and stood guard at the school bus doors.

Patrick was a kind African American man in his twenties. Patrick was normally quiet and very caring. He would drive any route without question to the best of his ability.

As the ambulance arrived and the paramedics collected their equipment, the child was still unconscious as the Director held the child in his arms and kept her airway clear.

Patrick opened the school bus doors and let the paramedics on board. As the paramedic stood in the aisle waiting to assess the young student, Patrick provided the initial information and explained the child's current condition.

Patrick talked with the children still seated on the school bus and consoled them while the paramedics worked on the child.

"Rosa is going to be fine, guys!" he quietly said. "She is just taking a quick nap…she wasn't feeling well!"

As the Director finished providing first aid and passed over the emergency care to the paramedics, he headed towards a large group of parents who were standing outside the school bus doors.

The police officer had the parents form a line, and each presented their identification to have their child released from the school bus.

One mother was extremely angry as she was told she could not have her child until she presented her identification.

The Director continued to verify the parents identification and released the children as the angry mother drove back to her apartment to get her purse.

As the paramedics took the young child to their ambulance, the kids still on the school bus were all watching with concern.

"Where did the parents come from, Patrick?" the Director asked.

"Most are from the apartments." Patrick answered, "I know the kids have been texting them on their phones too!"

"You got to love technology!"

"I am proud of you, Patrick!" the Director said. "You did it right today!"

The school bus erupted. The students began clapping, and Patrick dropped his head.

You know, sometimes bus drivers don't want a round of applause. We just want our kids to be safe. We want parents to be confident we are trying our very best.

Driving in busy traffic or adverse road conditions, we skillfully keep a very large vehicle on the road. Our training and experience over the years hone our skills to drive under stressful situations, keep everyone safe and sound, and protect everyone's precious children.

This emergency was a significant emotional event for everyone involved.

They take pride in their profession and appreciate words of affirmation.

"Sometimes, I truthfully wish people could take a moment and acknowledge how difficult transporting children really is before they jump on social media or shout obscenities at a bus driver," a bus driver shouted during a safety meeting.

"People have no idea how awesome our bus drivers are until you see one in action!", the Director exclaimed.

Patrick left our school district to work across the county closer to his parents. His father became ill and Patrick wanted to be closer to take care of him and his mother.

We miss him. We were blessed to have such an amazing man work for our school district driving a school bus.

During our end-of-year celebration, we had a farewell for Patrick and sent him off with a giant basket of movies, popcorn, and candy. Patrick was a movie buff.

Patrick talked about how much he loved going to the movies when he was not driving a school bus. Patrick could talk about movies all day long, especially murder mysteries!

Chapter 15
A Watchful Eye

Providing children with a pleasant experience on the school bus can be a full-time job. Leticia is unbelievably skilled at entertaining her children while driving them back and forth to school.

Leticia offers the best fist bumps and a treasure box full of toys and trinkets. Sometimes, she will have goodie bags on Fridays for her children following the bus rules.

Leticia has not submitted a discipline report on her school bus in years. Her children are well-behaved, even when Leticia is absent, and a substitute driver is behind the wheel. You see, Leticia brings a specific set of skills to work each day most drivers don't have in their repertoire.

Leticia brings creativity, kindness, humor, empathy, joy, and an array of items that her children enjoy. She has a mini library, a box of toys, and a treasure box full of things you might find in a dentist's office after finishing your annual teeth cleaning. She employs these things to effectively communicate with her children. Some enjoy receiving a gift for their good behavior, while others appreciate her words of affirmation. You can easily see the kids really love Ms. Leticia!

The parents who have children riding Leticia's school bus often praise her over the phone, on social media, and in person at district activities.

Leticia is happily married and has four children of her own. They are all grown and living independently. Driving a school bus full of children may bring fond memories back for

Leticia. I know she is always talking about her kids on her school bus.

I'll bet Leticia's adult children remember their childhood and probably talk to their own children about how awesome she was to be their parent.

Bus drivers give their best every day to show their children they are always going to be there when they need them. In the morning or the afternoon, the same smiling face will be there to give a child a fist bump in the morning and ask them how their day was at school in the afternoon.

It doesn't seem like a big deal, except some children head home to chaos, an empty house, or an empty refrigerator.

There are places within our school district where families live in substandard conditions. Families struggle to find a way to keep food on the table, the lights on, and their kids safe.

Parents struggle with alcohol and drug addiction, spouses incarcerated, and little or no income. We see children running free without any direction or parental supervision. We have some parents who are abusive or simply have no compassion for their own children.

For bus drivers, we pick children up and smile as we take them to school each day. Dropping children off at home in a hostile environment is always hard.

We know when our kids are going straight into harm's way or when they are suffering from total neglect.

"I cannot tell you how many times I have sat my spouse down and asked her if we could adopt a child!" a driver exclaimed to the coordinator and the special education director. "It is just not fair to the child!"

"It breaks my heart to know a child's next meal might be at school on Monday morning," a driver said, "I have tried to give them snacks and drinks to get them through the weekend."

It is easy to see when a child's parents are not focused on taking care of their babies. Pulling up to a stop, I see an emaciated horse kept inside a small pen no bigger than a basketball court, without any hay or water to drink.

Three mangy dogs are barking through the gate. The student's father is sitting on the porch drinking a cheap beer and smoking a cigarette.

My student jumps off the bus, opens the gate, and runs past the dogs. His father yells at him to close the gate as I pull away.

We think these things are incomprehensible. But, for children who live in these conditions daily, it is normal.

Children are resilient and can overcome most adversity. Working in student transportation, we still have a duty to report and protect our children. Getting them help is a tough task when their parents do not believe they deserve it.

Chapter 16
Silent Smile

Last year, I was assigned to drive a special education bus for a driver who was out sick. Normally, I drive my assigned route; however, the Director asked for me to take a look at the conditions of a child's home I was transporting. He knows I am candid and will provide the details he needs to submit a report.

I started the school bus and headed to the high school to pick up some children from the special education unit. There are some students who are above the age of graduation and continue at attend high school to learn life skills until they are as old as 23 years old. It is a great program to help our young disabled adults get on their feet and be productive in the workplace and at home.

One female child, who quietly sat in her seat, bumping her head against the window, quickly gained my attention. According to the case paperwork, she was one of seven children in a single household. She was raised by her Grandmother and her father in substandard living conditions.

Her name was Angelica Sanchez. She was 18 years old and was a low-functioning autistic child. Angelica was non-verbal, and I was told she was a "runner".

A runner simply means we have to make sure we release the child to a parent, sibling, or guardian because the child will take off running, sometimes right into traffic.

As I approached Angelica's home, I remembered what the diagnostician said about Angelica and her living conditions. When evaluating students for support, everything that is relevant is annotated in a meeting to provide a holistic view of the student's entire situation.

An evaluation provides information about their life at home, at school, and even on the school bus. Typically, when a special meeting is conducted for a child in need, everyone in the room works together to see how best they can help a student.

Ms. Simko, the diagnostician, told me the child was living with grandma next door for most of her life. Grandma had recently passed away, and the child was staying with the father and her six brothers.

When I pulled up, I opened the doors and Angelica would not get off the school bus. She looked at me and tears began streaming down her cheeks. The father came to the school bus and her older brother stood on the porch. I had a feeling something was wrong. I could tell she feared something.

After Angelica finally got off the school bus, I continued driving the route wondering what was going on with the child.

I drove the same route for several days, watching what was happening on the school bus and when I dropped Angelica off. I asked the diagnostician if there was any indication of wrongdoing going on, and she became very quiet.

Under Federal Law, I had no reason to know about Angelica's previous situation, as a school bus driver. As a parent, I could tell something was wrong.

After a week or so, I noticed Angelica was no longer riding the school bus. For days, I worried something terrible had happened to Angelica.

I learned a week later, she was being physically abused by her oldest brother. Thankfully, Child Protective Services made sure Angelica and her five younger brothers were taken under the care of the State.

The oldest brother was arrested for a previous crime and was now in jail. He had robbed a local business.

The investigator who handled the investigation filed charges against the older brother for the abuse of his sister, Angelica.

As bus drivers, we are all protectors of the children we transport everyday. We will stand tall and protect those who cannot protect themselves. I am proud to say Angelica is safe now, and I will always remember her situation.

I distinctly remember the very first time I met Angelica. She smiled and seemed happy to be on the school bus. This was months before the investigation.

I hope Angelica can smile again in the near future. I am relieved to know she is safe.

Chapter 17
Going to the Zoo

Field trips are an absolute blast if you get the right one. With a bus full of elementary teachers and students, we departed for the zoo with our bagged lunches, water bottles, and backpacks.

Ms. Johns, a third-grade teacher at Manor Elementary, asks the children to sit three to a seat. Student instructions are over-modulated and very easy to understand.

The children walk in line like little toy soldiers, following the commands of their teachers. As they sit down, you can tell they are excited about riding the school bus, since most do not ride the school bus daily.

Sitting in my seat, I can't even see the children in my mirror. Our seats are much higher from the floor than one would assume. I can hear lots of commotion, though!

"Is everyone ready to go to the zoo?" I ask as I walk down the aisle.

"Yes!" children cheer.

"How many of you would like to see a tiger?"

Several children raise their hands.

"How many of you would like to see a gorilla?" I said with enthusiasm.

Several hands raised. "How about you…what would you like to see?" I asked a small boy sitting quietly.

"A snake," he replied quietly.

"Oh, a snake you say?" I happily replied.

"They have big ones and little ones for you to see, don't worry!" I explained.

"Alright kids, stay seated and we will be at the zoo before you know it!" I said as I walked towards the front of the bus.

Our ride was about 45 minutes.

We pulled up to the zoo parking lot, and I dropped the children off at the entrance with their teachers.

I pulled away and headed to the large vehicle parking area to secure my school bus. I personally love the zoo!

I love the animals, the beautiful gardens, and of course, the concessions.

"Bad food is always the best recipe for good times!"

I paid my entry fee and headed to the African Safari section to feed the giraffes and get a cold lemonade. I watched the teachers leading their small groups out into the different areas to explore.

The lead teacher exchanged phone numbers with me so I could have the bus cooled down and ready to roll when the kids were finished visiting the zoo.

As I enjoyed the beautiful animals and embraced the wonderful weather, I walked past the petting zoo area. Two groups were taking our students to pet the animals.

They had a domestic farm animal section on one side and a lady zookeeper with a large iguana in her arms on the other.

Our kids and other visitors watched in amazement as she fed the iguana and talked about him. His tail went past her waist, and he didn't seem to mind the attention.

I continued past the petting zoo and walked down the ramp towards the new aquatic exhibit. "Lots of people for such a small exhibit!" I said to a zoo employee.

"We just opened it this Spring!" a zoo employee replied.

After walking through the vibrant aquariums and circling around into a large stone foyer, I saw another group of our children leaning over an open aquarium and petting little stingrays and touching starfish.

"How cool is that!" I exclaimed.

Ms. Andrews was taking pictures as the children were mesmerized by the experience. Some were playing in the water. Others were touching the stingrays. There was a little girl who seemed terrified at the very sight. She wasn't having it at all!

Lunch was approaching, and you know bus drivers love to eat! I headed to the concession stand to work on my "see food" diet.

Grabbing a couple of burgers, some fries, and another large lemonade, I was happy as a bug in a rug watching people walking by from exhibit to exhibit.

There is nothing better than bringing children on a field trip where you can see discovery in their eyes. You are part of a child seeing something for the very first time!

Honestly, I don't know how the teachers stay so calm and patient throughout the entire day. As I waited patiently, the heat is definitely noticeable, but a breeze makes everything almost bearable.

Before you know it, it is time to head back to my school bus and cool it off before our ride home. As I settle into my seat, I take a moment and reflect on an absolutely beautiful day as I take a sip of my watered-down lemonade.

Bringing the bus around to the entrance, our elementary students looked tired! The teachers guided their students onto their assigned school buses. Once on board, each teacher began checking off every child from their list.

Ms. Johns finished her list, announced we were leaving, and sat down with a long sigh of relief. She had a hard day, for sure!

As we pulled into the elementary school, most children were sound asleep. Under normal circumstances, napping on the school bus is encouraged as long as riders don't miss their stop.

Right now, we have to figure out how to wake all these children, move them inside the school, and prepare them for the upcoming dismissal to go home.

"Alright everybody!" I sang to our sleepy children, "It's time to go...the trip is over!"

"I hope you had fun...our trip is done!" I continued singing.

I continued singing until every child exited. Smiling and thanking them for going to the zoo. Most said thank you in their little voices. Some rubbed their eyes and followed the child in front of them. All of them were exhausted.

Ms. Johns offered her appreciation and said, "I enjoyed our time together."

She walked down the steps, turned around and smiled.

"It was my absolute pleasure, Ms. Johns!" I responded.

I headed back to the bus barn to prepare for my afternoon route.

Chapter 18
Ham and Cheese

Sandra, a bus driver originally from Baton Rouge, Louisiana, reported a fight on her bus over the two-way radio a few weeks ago. Normally, Sandra is cool and calm; but, this situation was much different. She sounded deeply frustrated over the radio and our dispatcher immediately sent our Director out to help her.

When there is a significant incident, our Director or Coordinator will often drive out to the location and meet the school bus driver to try to resolve the situation.

During a safety meeting, we all listened as Sandra explained the entire incident in detail.

"When our director arrived at my school bus, I was parked on an old country road canopied by beautiful oak trees." Sandra explained.

"A young, male middle school student made some rude comments about another student who was seated in the back of the school bus." She continued.

"The offended student came up to address the situation and proceeded to punch the rude school student straight in his nose." Sandra explained.

"With little or no experience in the octagon, the bloodied student grasped the t-shirt of his new best friend and initiated a tug and pull move accompanied by a request for parlay."

"As the two pushed each other back and forth, a nearby student decided to take the golden opportunity to initiate a food fight on my school bus!" she enthusiastically declared.

Since it was the last day of school, one would guess the kids figured there would be no disciplinary action as a consequence for anything they chose to do on the last day of school riding home.

Actually, for one to further explain the intensity of the situation and the pure potential of mischievous behavior, I must elaborate.

You see, the last day of school is an early release day for all students. Aside from cleaning up classrooms and having end-of-year parties, the child nutrition department makes sure every student has lunch to eat when they get home.

The lunch ladies make bag lunches for all of the students to take home. Now, let's do the math!

Bag lunches can be identified as a ham slice and cheese slice between two pieces of bread plus an irresistible opportunity to have a bit of fun equals perfect ammunition that verifies the target has been hit by sticking to one's face.

Just apply mustard or mayonnaise to make things really interesting!

"The first male perpetrator disassembled his ham and cheese sandwich and proceeded to whip the ham slice across the aisle, subsequently slapping the side of a female student's face and dropping into her lap."

Some bus drivers started to chuckle while others shook their head in disgust.

"Immediately following the initial attack, the female student showed her appreciation for the ham across her cheek by sending small carrots with across the school bus doused in ranch dressing.

In the end, seven students engaged in the food fight with multiple casualties and noteworthy collateral damage.

Now, let's fast forward.

"Where are my fighters?" our Director addressed the entire school bus of students upon his arrival and stepping on the school bus.

A bloody nose popped up over the seat, "Right here."

After a second hail, both middle school boys shamefully walked forward and were asked to step off the school bus to discuss their wrongdoing.

Immediately following his discussion with the two grapplers, he had both boys call their parents to come to pick them up.

"Riding on the school bus is a privilege. When you fight, you make things dangerous for everyone," he explained to the remaining students on the school bus.

"Our two fighters will not be continuing the bus ride home today!" he added.

"Now, I understand there are several students who have decided to be disrespectful and throw food on the school bus..." he said, "your actions are unacceptable and will not be tolerated!"

Everyone on the school bus peered over their seats and listened.

"You all know cameras don't lie. You also know this is the very last day of school." he continued.

"I am going to give you one chance to be responsible for your actions."

"If you make me take the time to review the cameras to find out who was throwing the food, your consequences are going to be much more severe!"

It didn't take long. He convinced seven students to admittedly and shamefully walk forward. The Director told them to sit in the first two rows as they reached the front of the school bus.

"Your bus driver works very hard to take care of this school bus and keep you safe to and from school," he scolded the mischievous students.

"Today, you are all going to apologize to Ms. Sandra as a consequence. You will do so individually, and it better be sincere!" the Director explained.

Sandra explained to our drivers, "The very first child didn't do half bad with his apology."

"Sorry, that's not going to work," the Director interrupted.

"Let me explain this to you once again in simplest terms." he reiterated. "Your apologies to Ms. Sandra better be good!"

"Don't make me resort to calling your parents." He stated.

As the children apologized, one by one, the apologies increased in quality and creativity as each child tried to make their apology sincere and believable.

Some attempted to "one up" the child before them.

"Ms. Sandra, I am so sorry for throwing the carrots," a student said, "I will never do it again and I know that you work really hard to keep us safe!"

"I am so very, very ,very sorry," the last student finally finished.

Most of the quality apologies included sad eyes and humble body language. Dramatic, to say the least.

"They really poured it on!" Sandra continued. "I was not sure how the Director kept a straight face during the entire apology session."

"I struggled to not laugh as the apologies got longer and longer!" she explained.

Immediately following the scolding, the kids were strongly encouraged to pick up the food and debris off the floor, the seats, and each other.

They quickly scrambled to clean up the bus and brought the food and debris up to the front of the bus to the trash can.

Honestly, they just wanted to get rid of this man who could potentially call their parents and mess up their summer break plans.

Our two middle school fighters were greeted by the school resource officers and their parents as we pulled away.

Everyone watched through the windows as the police officers talked to them. I am sure every child wondered what happened to those two boys.

Chapter 19
Handle the Truth

On television, you might remember a famous movie where a custodian explains to a teacher how he hears and sees everything that goes on in their high school.

Consider the possibility that your children may not tell you everything or they may struggle sometimes with the telling truth.

Not my child, you say?

Too many times our children are bamboozling school faculty and staff and even their own parents when they are not following rules.

They can tell some creative and convincing stories, far from the truth, just to save their own hide.

However, cameras catch a great deal. But not everything. There is another way to find out the truth.

School faculty and staff spend all year building strong relationships with their students. Sometimes taking positive relationships and treating them as a valuable resource can help finding out the truth.

Every day, upstanding students bring incidents on their cell phones straight to the bus drivers, cafeteria workers, custodians, coaches, secretaries, and teachers.

They provide first-hand accounts of things happening on campus to help stop them. Students care about their school and cherish having a safe environment to learn.

It's funny, our kids know more that's going on than we give them credit. Besides, most kids grow tired of the troublemakers, the bullies, and the relentless harassment around campus, especially the high school students.

Children raised with strong beliefs and values can undoubtedly be a great resource. Instilling integrity and personal courage can produce upstanding students.

"I refuse to allow my students to use the word "snitch" on my school bus," a seasoned bus driver explained during a department meeting, "I tell them only criminals and police use the word "snitch," and they shouldn't be afraid to tell the truth!"

"Integrity is our greatest value in life," another bus driver exclaimed.

Although we all try to teach our kids right from wrong, they often need us to make decisions on the things they face throughout the school day.

Kids often come to us and ask for advice. We try to keep our advice to a minimum and try to empower their parents. Sometimes, it is a child's simple conversation with you where they really want to know the answer to something and we become their mentor.

"I was eating my lunch, and Billy kept making fun of me and the way I was eating," Grace explained. Grace is a third-grade student from Manor Elementary School.

"Billy keeps making me feel sad when I go to lunch. I have to sit by him, and he makes me miserable," she continued.

"Did you tell your teacher?" I asked.

"No," she answered, "that might make it worse!"

"Grace, you should be able to eat your lunch without Billy making you feel sad every day," I said.

"I know." she replied.

"Will you think about telling your teacher, Ms. Johnson, what is going on at lunch?" I asked.

"I guess," Grace responded as she appeared to think it over.

"When you tell someone who can help," I explained. "it may seem uncomfortable at first, but standing up for yourself can make you feel so much better!"

"Ok, I will tell her today!" Grace said as she smiled.

"I am so proud of you, Grace!" I said. "Let me know how it goes this afternoon when I pick you up to go home!"

She smiled and nodded her head in approval. She looked out the window and seemed to be content with my response.

Our role as bus drivers extends across campuses, into homes, and into the future. Last year, we had a high school graduate request her bus driver to assist with the formalities of her graduation.

As an honored graduate, she shared her admiration for her bus driver in her speech as she explained his impact on her life and how she cherished his patience, understanding, and genuine kindness over the years she rode his school bus.

"I believe our discussions on the school bus encouraged me to focus on my grades, stay out of trouble, and become the person I am." She said in front of her graduating class, family members, and graduation attendees.

"Mr. Jim was my coach and my mentor, not just my bus driver. He gave me the strength to stand up for myself, believe in myself, to set goals, and accomplish them!"

Our entire department watched the recorded ceremony with great pride during our district end of year convocation.

The Superintendent recognized Mr. Jim in front of the entire school district. After his kind words and a standing ovation, Mr. Jim returned to his seat with tears in his eyes.

Chapter 20
Technology is Key

I was talking to the Principal while we were waiting for the children to be dismissed outside the middle school. He explained in detail how he uses social media platforms and applications in his investigations.

"Our students are constantly on their smartphones, and they have access to just about anything," he said.

"Students are so technically savvy anymore. Most parents really struggle to understand basic technology." he continued, "Kids are able to access applications on their smartphones, and honestly, they are really good at hiding things they don't want Mom or Dad to see!"

"I try to throw little bits of technical information and know-how to indicate I understand technology as much as the kids do," he said. "You can see the kids quickly realize my level of technical understanding, and they start to believe they are unable to lie to me."

It seemed to me like the Principal could get the truth when nobody else could. His technological understanding is what strengthens his resolve when addressing student discipline. I enjoyed talking with him and learning about his disciplinary process and his technological expertise. I asked several questions myself!

I am sure addressing student discipline is difficult without having an array of resources to support investigations. Some kids always try to manipulate the situation to their benefit when they are in trouble.

We try to treat every school bus as a learning environment. In a regular classroom, assistant principals handle student discipline and teachers teach.

As bus drivers, we don't yell at children or try to punish them for their actions on the school bus. We try to teach, coach, and encourage them to do the right thing.

When we have students who refuse to follow the rules, we try to remind them of the rules, talk with their parents, or when everything else has failed, we ask for help from the school leadership.

Sometimes, we can't help but be a bit frustrated when it seems like our disciplinary reports are being ignored. I understand school administrators are really busy; but, we really need their help sometimes.

For example, I have a child on my school bus who enjoys screaming to hear himself.

Now, he sounds like a young girl, since he is only a sixth grader, and his voice hasn't really changed yet. But, this young man will scream unannounced and disturb my concentration in an instant. Thank goodness the scary movie casting manager hasn't met him yet. I'm sure he would be quite competitive in the next scary movie being filmed.

After asking the middle school assistant principal for more information concerning a disciplinary report I submitted for our young middle school student, I was told, "Sometimes, it is not what you think!"

I was intrigued by his comment and a bit eager to understand what the Assistant Principal meant.

"Could you explain what you mean?" I asked.

"Sure," he replied.

The Principal explained to me that children need to be evaluated holistically to determine the root of their problems. "Maybe the child sees adverse behaviors at home or is experiencing a major disruption," he said.

"Some children act out of character when their parents are fighting, arguing, or contemplating divorce, for instance."

"Really?" I said.

"Maybe a student is hungry and struggling to get to their next meal because there is nothing to eat at home," he continued.

"You would be amazed at how many of our children rely on breakfast and lunch in school cafeterias because their family is so poor and cannot afford to prepare three meals a day," he continued.

"Don't forget children may have mental or physical disabilities to consider as well," he sadly explained.

"Sometimes adverse behavior indicates an underlying problem." he explained.

"We have students that have incarcerated parents, parents who have passed away. They may be subject to a court decision that removes them from their homes and places them into the foster care system," he added.

"All of the children I mentioned have to go to school somewhere," he said.

"Every child still needs to be loved." I added.

"Absolutely, our counselors, teachers, behavior specialists, social workers, coaches, and administrators are at the forefront of our children's lives," he said, "Our bus drivers, custodians, and lunch ladies play a critical role in caring for them as well!"

We continued chatting about different students and how I could better support them. I still find the screaming distracting; but, I have a new understanding and I am willing to try new things to get him to change his behavior.

You could tell the assistant principal genuinely cared about his students.

I believe he honestly tries his best to help kids!

Chapter 21
Happy Holidays

Sometimes, we see the funniest things happen in the transportation community. During the holidays, my coordinator received a call from a campus principal at Alexander Elementary.

According to the Principal, a student's father was in the main office asking for assistance from the campus and the transportation department. The father was deeply concerned as it was only a few days until Christmas.

Some families set up their trees after Thanksgiving and decorate their homes for the holidays. As Christmas approaches and Santa gets ready to make his rounds, some families begin placing gifts under the tree to be opened on Christmas day.

This father was concerned because Christmas was right around the corner and he noticed there were several gifts missing from under their Christmas tree.

He asked his wife and his older son if they had moved the gifts, and both had no idea the gifts were even missing, much less moved them.

He looked across his living room, and his little kindergartner was standing by the Christmas tree with her head dropped and her hands behind her back, swaying back and forth.

The father walked into the living room, sat down on the couch, and quietly asked his daughter to come over so he could ask her a question.

"Where did the presents go, Elizabeth?" he asked.

She stuck her three fingers in her mouth and mumbled in response. Her eyes began to well up with tears.

"Did you hide the presents?" he asked calmly.

Elizabeth shook her head from side to side.

"Please tell me what happened, sweetie!" he kindly asked as he consoled her.

After several attempts and his wife joining the inquiry, it turns out Ms. Elizabeth had taken some gifts, placed them in her backpack, and passed them out on the school bus.

Elizabeth's father, a mechanic at the local dealership, wanted to know who had received these holiday gifts so he could independently contact the recipient's parents to request they be returned.

Restricted from divulging personal information, the main office secretary offered to contact each child's parent and help return the Christmas gifts back under the tree.

Throughout the afternoon, the secretary successfully managed to contact every child's parent who received an early Christmas gift, and do you know she asked each parent to bring them to the main office and they actually did?

Every parent smiled as they brought the gifts back. Priceless holiday stories ensued as they dropped off the gifts. The guidance counselor contacted the father, and he thankfully picked up the gifts and praised the office staff for their efforts.

Everyone found the situation hilarious. Everyone was happy to help with the father's desperate search. I am sure the father will tell this story for years to come.

Elizabeth's concept of gift-giving and sweetness led to an array of people smiling, sharing stories, and turning a desperate situation into acts of grace and kindness.

Her holiday spirit was everlasting.

Chapter 22
Mentorship

Driving a school bus can be emotionally taxing on any normal human being. In the Spring, I had just begun my afternoon route, and my students were quiet and content.

Two students started arguing in the back of the school bus and after several reminders, I told them to stop or they would be moved to the front of the school bus.

As you would imagine, a student being told to move to the front of the bus away from their friends is the ultimate punishment in our eyes.

Unfortunately, it is a dual punishment.

Parents will call the transportation office and ask for their children to be moved to the front in lieu of being suspended off the school bus. Our parents actually believe this method solves all school bus disciplinary infractions.

We love to accommodate requests; however, this can prove to be difficult when you already have the first three rows filled with kids with challenging behaviors.

Moving them up is sometimes not the best solution to the behavior problem.

Think about it. What child do you know actually feels punished when they are suspended from the school bus? Not our children.

They want to hang out with Mom and Dad!

So, one could assume this punishment is actually for the parent themselves. Why are we punishing the parent?

The parents of suspended children have to drive their kids to school, use extra gasoline and take time out of their busy day. When administrators suspend bus privileges, the very first response from the parent is to request a seat change versus suspension.

Truthfully, moving a student to the front of the bus is a social nightmare. Every other child on the school bus walks past them, knowing they are in trouble. They cannot sit with their friends or get away with anything.

Suddenly, riding the school bus is an awful experience; but, seat changes are almost always made by the bus driver prior to any disciplinary referral. This consequence is reserved for minor infractions.

Standing on my soap box, I have to ask those who want their kids back on the bus after being suspended only one question. Do you put your kids in the front seat when they do not listen?

Let's talk about the collateral damage from this decision?

Instead of talking with their friends, they are now talking to their bus driver. Tirelessly talking about everything and anything, about their friends, their favorite color, and how one actually operates a school bus safely.

People, you have now punished the school bus driver!

"Don't get me wrong, we love your children!" Take a moment and recall an experience where you are trying to follow directions on your cell phone to an important engagement, and your son or daughter is talking about what little Johnny said in class this morning about dinosaurs and how they have feathers like birds!

Now, get behind the wheel of a 40-foot yellow school bus, filled to the rim with elementary students in rush hour traffic, and try to pay attention to the road.

Suddenly, feathers on a dinosaur are no longer important.

Better yet, I respectfully request you do not complain when I drive past a bus stop because I was concentrating on the pudding they served in the cafeteria this afternoon, not having whipped cream on top!

These are valid concerns our children have throughout the course of their day, and because they haven't had a chance to vent, they are talking to me!

"How dare the cafeteria ladies forget the whipped cream... seriously!"

Allison Cobb can share some of the greatest scientific lessons learned from Mr. Kowick, her science teacher. You see, Allison loves to tell me about her day. I absolutely enjoy listening, and I try to be as attentive as I can since she goes home to an empty house every day.

Now, if I put Jeffrey Borden up front, Allison cannot get a word in edgewise. That is a long afternoon, let me tell ya!

What happened to disciplinary consequences at school or being grounded at home?

They say parenting includes telling your children no and holding them accountable for their actions. It is easier to take their cell phone or send them to their room; but, talking to them about why they did something or asking them what they would do differently in the same situation next time might yield greater benefits in their development and understanding.

After all, your children are amazing and they do make mistakes. Teaching them life's lessons is actually our pleasure.

Often, we find more humor in the kids' adverse behavior than upset. After all, they are just kids!

Chapter 23
Driving in the Snow

As a young man, I have spent a lot of time on the school bus. I remember my bus driver and always respected her authority. My parents were divorced and my mother worked from early morning until late in the evening every day.

I was essentially a "latchkey" kid.

I just turned fifty years old, and I still vividly remember Ms. Marion taking us back and forth to school every day. She was a silent professional and never yelled. As a matter of fact, Ms. Marion rarely talked.

She smiled when we got on the school bus as I walked back to my seat. Sometimes, I would take a late bus home because of athletic practices and she would be driving the activity bus as well. Ms. Marion made sure I got to and from school without a hitch.

Riding the activity bus, as they called it, was an evening norm for me. I played different sports throughout the school year and spent more time at school than at home.

As a latchkey kid, my bus driver talked to me individually and checked on me a lot. She was kind and I gave her more respect than my own parents. Having divorced parents made things really hard because they were rarely around.

Ms. Marion drove our school bus my entire childhood, and I remember her like it was yesterday. One day, Ms. Marion was picking up the high school students on her early route.

I was in junior high school and it was December. The snow outside was beautiful and the roads had not been plowed. My sister and the older kids from the neighborhood got on the school bus around 7am headed to the high school which was around 25 miles away.

The weather was terrible, and the crosswinds made it difficult to see. My family lived at the very top of a steep hill in Western Pennsylvania. The roads were snow-covered and regardless of the road salt the borough dropped on the roads, Ms. Marion had to negotiate through the treacherous weather with bad road conditions regardless.

As the school bus crested the hill and started down a half-mile decline, Ms. Marion tapped her brakes, decelerated her bus and made it to a second stop, a short distance down the hill. As she came to a stop, the tires slid past the bus stop. Some children turned around and headed home, knowing the possibility of a possible accident.

The students from the top of the hill, still on board the school bus, were getting ready for the ride of their lives. As Ms. Marion attempted to decelerate and tap her brakes down the hill over a half mile long, the bus eventually lost traction.

The school bus began to increase speed as she headed straight down the hill toward the American Legion, which was a three-story, large brick building.

Skillfully adjusting her foot from the brake to the accelerator, Ms. Marion regained traction and changed direction across an open parking lot, narrowly missing the American Legion.

Instead of hitting the American Legion head-on, Ms. Marion steered her way between the two massive buildings, avoiding certain death.

The school bus pulverized two telephone poles as it slid across the main thoroughfare. Since the main road was treated, she actually regained traction, and the school bus spun 180 degrees and slammed into the local meat market. Finally coming to a stop, the back end of the school bus hung over a small creek below.

Three kids in the back of the school bus sustained minor injuries. Ms. Marion was hospitalized for several days. My sister and her friends lived to see another day.

From that day forward, nobody ever doubted Ms. Marion's ability to drive a school bus. As an adult, I question the use of chains on the bus tires; but, this was almost forty years ago. Who knows what safety equipment was available at the time.

My entire life, I have genuinely appreciated Ms. Marion and her valiant effort that day. She clearly saved my sister's life and the other children on the school bus. She spent quite a few days in the hospital.

When she returned, we all thanked Ms. Marion for being so awesome. I can say, not a single parent sued the school district or insinuated Ms. Marion had done anything less than save the lives of her students.

She was and may always be our hero.

Chapter 24
I Can Do It

They say learning how to drive a school bus starts with driving big vehicles. After a school district makes sure you're healthy enough to drive a school bus and the Department of Transportation agrees, anyone can start to get their commercial driver's permit.

If you didn't know, school districts typically conduct criminal background checks and request motor vehicle reports in the hiring process for every bus driver. Nobody wants to be on the 6 o'clock news explaining they hired a criminal to drive their kids around town.

Public school districts check, check, and re-check before they put you or anyone else around kids much less driving school buses.

After you survive the rigorous background checks, complete a ridiculous physical examination performing an array of comical tasks, and watch a million videos, you can move forward to learning how to drive a school bus.

So, you have your driver's permit, and a medical card and have received all the safety training you can stomach. Now, it's time to meet with the trainers.

These are the people who will explain every part of a school bus and show you how to drive kids around town safely, back up and even parallel park.

"Ladies and Gentlemen, please find me one single school bus driver on earth who will actually willingly parallel park a school bus anywhere!"

Moving on.

As your training continues with air brake tests, turning a thousand times, and reciting railroad crossing procedures, most drivers start to build confidence.

"I can do this!" you say to yourself.

Then, your trainer tells you that you are ready to take your road test. You are staring at a certified examiner and you spend the next 45 minutes going over everything you learned pointing out each piece or part you supposed to check before you leave.

Moving past your perfected skills of backing up and parallel parking, you start up the bus and head out into the wild, blue yonder with your examiner and his handy, dandy clipboard. Excited as you pull out of the training area, you almost hit your first curb.

You try not to acknowledge it, and you continue to be absolutely focused on the prize.

Left turn, right turn, railroad crossing, and a traffic circle.

You pull back into the bus lot knowing you did it! The examiner says the words you have been waiting for all day.

"Congratulations, you passed!"

As you flex your muscles in the breakroom upon your return, nobody seems to care except for the dispatcher, who knows she needs to put you on a route as soon as yesterday.

After all, no transportation department ever has enough bus drivers!

Now, my friend. You are ready to drive a school bus.

A final thought as you prepare to drive your kids for the first time. Remember, bus drivers are a special group of people.

When people ask what type of person gets up to drive a school bus at the crack of dawn, takes a few hours off, and comes back to drive the same route at dinner time, I can only try to explain it.

So, let me tell you.

Bus drivers are a proud group of folks who care about each other and about their kids. They argue about how you park, race to see who arrives first on campus, and whine about what was said on the two-way radio.

But, when things get busy, they work together like a well-oiled machine. Everyone works together to get every single child where they need to be on time and safely.

Most bus drivers try to run a tight ship. They do their best to keep everyone seated, situated, and content. They work with parents, teachers, administrators, and other fellow drivers to ensure their children have everything they need.

I met our Superintendent and he shared his admiration for bus drivers and the service they provide to our school district. He humbly explained his fond memories as a kid riding the school bus. As a bus driver, I am proud to know my Superintendent, our campus administrators, and our local community appreciate what we do every day for kids.

I love my job.

We all do.

Made in the USA
Monee, IL
18 November 2024

70410390R00079